TXT 870 0017

OVID

METAMORPHOSES VIII

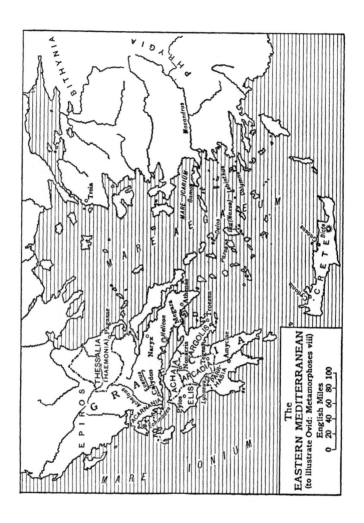

The
EASTERN MEDITERRANEAN
(to illustrate Ovid: Metamorphoses viii)

English Miles
0 20 40 60 80 100

BITHYNIA

PHRYGIA

Maeandrus

Troia

MARE ICARIUM

Samos

A

E

MARE

G

A

E

Labinthus

calymne

U

M

Naxos(Dia)

Delos

Paros

CRETE

Gnosus

Dicte

Phaestus

THESSALIA
(HAEMONIA)   Pagasae

EPIROS

G

R

A

Naryx

Helicon

Megara

Athenae

Nonacris

ACARNANIA   Calydon

Achelous   ACHAIA

Evenus

Echinades   Pylos   ELIS

ARCADIA

Troezen

ARGOLIS

Tegea

Lycaeus   PARR-   Amyclae

HASIA

MARE   IONIUM

OVID

METAMORPHOSES VIII

Edited with Introduction, Notes
and Vocabulary by

H.E. Gould and J.L. Whiteley

Bristol Classical Press

Reprinted 2008 by
Bristol Classical Press, an imprint of
Gerald Duckworth & Co. Ltd.
90-93 Cowcross Street, London EC1M 6BF
Tel: 020 7490 7300
Fax: 020 7490 0080
info@duckworth-publishers.co.uk
www.ducknet.co.uk

First published 1940 by Macmillan & Co Ltd
Lines 87, 131-133, 136-137 and 156
were omitted from this edition.

A catalogue record for this book is available
from the British Library

ISBN 978 1 85399 722 8

Printed and bound in Great Britain by
CPI Antony Rowe, Eastbourne

FOREWORD

THIS book of the Metamorphoses has been edited
upon the principles indicated in the foreword to the
first volume of the publishers' ' Modern School Clas-
sics ' ; that is, upon the assumption that the shorter
time now given to Latin in the Secondary Schools,
often no more than a three-year course of either four
or five lessons a week, has made desirable and necessary a new type of text-book, in which the notes
give the pupil considerably more direct help in his
preparation, while omitting much, of less immediate
value to him, that was proper to a more leisurely
age.

The notes of the present edition have been written
for pupils commencing the study of Latin verse, as
it is the authors' belief that in very many secondary
schools the pupil begins the preparation of his verse
set-book without any previous reading of Latin
poetry.

The text will be found to vary little from the
standard Teubner edition. A few lines, sufficiently

indicated by the marginal numbering, have been omitted on the score of unsuitability. One passage, often omitted in school editions, it has not been thought necessary to exclude.

H. E. G.

WELLINGBOROUGH,   J. L. W.

NORTHANTS,

1940.

CONTENTS

LIST OF ILLUSTRATIONS

INTRODUCTION

(i) The Life of Ovid

THE Latin poet whom we know as Ovid—his full name was Publius Ovidius Naso—was born, in 43 B.C., during the first civil war that followed the assassination of Julius Caesar. His birthplace was Sulmo, now Sulmona, a town of central Italy, some ninety odd miles from Rome. He came of a good and wealthy family, belonging to the Equestrian order, the class of rich men ranking immediately below the Senatorial order, men whom we sometimes call ' the Knights ', a term which well suggests their substantial position in the community.

The young Publius was given, together with his brother (exactly one year older than himself) the usual education of the Roman leisured classes, whose young men mostly entered political life, and commonly by way of the profession of law. In this education, rhetoric, that is the composition and delivery of elaborate speeches on set themes, formed the culminating part, and this training left an indelible mark on Ovid's writings. He tells us himself,—he is, for a Roman writer, very informative

THE SEA WALL AT CONSTANZA—FEBRUARY, 1940
(The 'Tomi' of Ovid's exile)

upon his personal history—that very early the appeal
to him of a literary career became supreme, and,
in spite of his father's practical protests,—' even
Homer left no money '—to that career he devoted
himself. He was relieved from the necessity of
earning his own living by his patrimony, no longer
requiring to be shared with his brother, who had
died young.

As a poet Ovid was voluminous, facile and, in the
Roman smart set, popular, and his life seems to
have been an easy and happy one, in spite of the
fact that his first two ventures in matrimony were
failures. With his third wife he seems to have
lived on terms of great domestic happiness.

In the year 8 A.D., at the age of 51, he had
completed, without however finally revising, his
most ambitious poem, the Metamorphoses, in fifteen
books. In the same year and without warning,
so far as we know, he was visited with complete
and final ruin, in the shape of an edict of banishment
from the Emperor Augustus, bidding him withdraw
from Rome to the town of Tomi or Tomis, now Constanza, on the Rumanian shores of the Black Sea.
It is not difficult to imagine the misery of such
lonely exile among uncultured people who spoke
a barbarous mixture of Greek and Scythian. The
dragging, rigorous winters too proved intolerable to

one born under the warm Italian sun. We do not know the real reason for Ovid's ruin. Revealing though he usually is about himself, he nowhere more than hints at the cause of his tragedy. Yet his offence—*error* he calls it—must have been grave, for not the most ignoble and obsequious appeals to Augustus brought mitigation of the sentence, while Tiberius, that Emperor's successor, remained equally obdurate. For ten years Ovid continued to write. At least he was not so crushed by misfortune as to abandon the practice of his craft.

Ovid died in 18 A.D., without further contact with wife, family or friends, save, no doubt at long intervals, the exchange of unhappy letters. His life of just over sixty years had coincided almost exactly with the transition from the dying republic to the established monarchy of Caesarism.

(ii) THE WRITINGS OF OVID

In addition to the Metamorphoses Ovid wrote a number of poems, the *Amores*, the *De Arte Amatoria*, the *Heroïdes*, the *Remedia Amoris,* in all of which the subject is love, the chief amusement, not taken too seriously, of the set in which he lived and for whom he wrote.

Later came the *Fasti*, a record of the festivals of the Roman year, month by month, of which however we possess only the first six books. The poem is extremely interesting and valuable for the light it throws on Roman antiquities and religion.

After his exile, the poet produced the *Tristia* and *Ex Ponto*—' Letters from the Black Sea ', nine books in all, containing descriptions of his life in banishment, complaints of his misery and loneliness and appeals to Augustus, couched in language of unseemly flattery, for reconsideration of his sentence.

(iii) THE METAMORPHOSES (' TRANSFORMATIONS ')

The subject of this, Ovid's most elaborate and ambitious work, is indicated by him thus in the opening lines of the first book :

> in nova fert animus mutatas dicere formas
> corpora.
> 'My mind inclines to tell of bodies changed into new forms.'

In the fifteen books of this long poem Ovid gathers together a vast number of Greek myths, in which the unifying thread is the Metamorphosis or changing of humans or demi-gods into other forms, those for instance of stars, trees, and birds. The poet's greatest quality is that of story-telling, and thus such a subject gave him quite the best opportunities of his literary career. He shows immense skill too in joining the tales one to another. The book has had very great influence on later literature, particularly on our own Elizabethans. It was translated into the rich English of the period by Golding, and through his version profoundly affected, among others, Shakespeare.

(iv) THE STORIES OF BOOK VIII

The present book contains the following myths.

Lines 1-151. Scylla, the daughter of Nisus, King of Megara, is changed into the sea-bird Ciris, and her father into an Osprey.

ll. 152-182. The crown of Ariadne, daughter of King Minos of Crete, is changed by Bacchus into a constellation.

ll. 182-235. Daedalus and his son Icarus fit wings to their bodies and emulate the flight of birds (not a true metamorphosis this).

ll. 236-259. Perdix, nephew of Daedalus, and hurled by him in envy from the Acropolis, is changed by Minerva into a partridge.

ll. 260-546. The sisters of Meleager, who with his mother Althaea and father Oeneus is involved in destruction after his slaying of the Calydonian boar, are changed by Diana into guinea-hens.

ll. 547-610. The river god Achelous tells Theseus and his companions, returning from the boar-hunt, how certain nymphs, having failed to honour him,

were changed into islands, and how Perimele, beloved by him, underwent a similar metamorphosis.

ll. 611-724. Lelex, a companion of Theseus, tells
how a peasant couple, Philemon and Baucis, honoured by the gods in their lifetime for their piety,
were changed in extreme age into trees.

ll. 725-884. Achelous tells how Erysichthon, for
his impiety, was smitten with insatiable hunger, how
his daughter, sold by him to procure the means of
obtaining food, was changed by Neptune at her own
entreaty into a man, and how she possessed there-
after the power of changing herself into a great
variety of shapes.

(v) THE METRE OF THE POEM

Most English verse consists of lines in which
stressed syllables alternate with unstressed, as for
example in the lines :

'The ploughman homeward plods his weary way
And leaves the world to darkness and to me.'

Such verse is called *accentual*.

The principle of Greek and Latin verse is different.
It is based on the rhythmical arrangement of long
and short syllables, the long syllables taking twice
as long to pronounce as the short. This system may
be compared with music, long syllables corresponding
to *crotchets* and short to *quavers*, one *crotchet* being

equal to two *quavers*. This type of verse is called *quantitative*.

Just as, to appreciate the rhythm of English verse, you are taught to *scan*, i.e. divide the lines into *feet* and mark the stress in each foot, so you must learn to scan Latin verse by a similar division into feet and by marking the syllables long (–) or short (◡). Not only is it necessary to do this in order to understand the construction of the verse and the musical qualities of the poetry, but the ability to do it is a great help in translation, by making it possible to distinguish words alike in spelling but different in *quantity*, for example pŏpŭlŭs, *people*, from pōpŭlŭs, *poplar tree*.

The verses of the Metamorphoses are called heroic hexameters. In this verse two kinds of feet, or bars, are found. One is the *dactyl*, a long syllable followed by two short syllables, the other, the *spondee*, two long syllables. Each line, or hexameter, contains six feet, the first four of which may be either dactyls or spondees, the fifth being almost always a dactyl, and the sixth a spondee. In place of this sixth foot spondee a trochee (–◡) is allowable.

Thus the scheme of the hexameter is as follows:

1	2	3	4	5	6
– ◡ ◡	– ◡ ◡	– ◡ ◡	– ◡ ◡	– ◡ ◡	– –
or – –	– –	– –	– –		– ◡

In the scansion of these lines, no account is taken of syllables at the close of a word *ending* in a vowel or an *m*, if they are followed immediately by a word *commencing* with a vowel or an *h*. Such a final syllable is said to be *elided*, ' struck out ', though it was more probably slurred in pronunciation. Thus in l. 5, which begins *ante exspectatum* the final *e* of *ante* is ignored in scanning.

A long syllable is one that contains a vowel long *by nature*, or a diphthong ; or one which though its vowel is naturally short, ends with two consonants.

A short syllable is one that contains a vowel short *by nature* and ends either with no consonant, or with only one.

The two consonants which have been mentioned as having the effect of lengthening a syllable need not both occur in the one word. Thus in line 1, the final syllable of *nitidum* is long, though the *u* is naturally short, because that *u* is followed by *m* and the *r* of *retegente*.

PROSODY.

The following information about the quantity of Latin syllables will be found useful.

A. Relating to all syllables.

All diphthongs are long, except before another vowel.

B

B. Relating to final syllables.

1. Final *a* is usually short.

Except

 (*a*) in the abl. sg. of 1st decl. nouns, e.g. *mensā* ;

 (*b*) in the 2nd sg. imperative active of 1st conjugation verbs, e.g. *amā* ;

 (*c*) in indeclinable words like *intereā, frustrā.*

2. Final *e* is usually short.

Except

 (*a*) in the abl. sg. of 5th decl. nouns, e.g. *aciē.*

 (*b*) in the 2nd sg. imperative active of 2nd conjugation verbs, e.g. *monē* ;

 (*c*) in adverbs formed from adjectives in *-us, -a, -um*, e.g. *pulchrē*. Note however *benĕ, malĕ.*

3. Final *i* is usually long.

Except in *mihi, tibi, sibi, ubi, ibi*, in which it may be long or short, and in *quasi, nisi.*

4. Final *o* is usually long.

Except in *modo, duo, ego.*

C. Final syllables of words of more than one syllable, ending in any single consonant other than *s*, are short.

Except

 (*a*) *dispăr* ;

 (*b*) in the perfects *iĭt* and *petiĭt.*

D. (i) Final *as*, *os*, *es*, are long.

Except

   (*a*) *compŏs*, *penĕs* ;

   (*b*) in nominatives singular in *es* of 3rd declension nouns (consonant stems) having
genitive sg. in -*ĕtis*, -*ĭtis*, -*idis* : e.g. *segĕs*,
milĕs, *obsĕs*. (But note *pariēs*, *abiēs*,
Cerēs.)

   (*c*) in compounds of *es* (from *sum*), e.g. *abĕs*,
prodĕs.

(ii) Final *us* and *is* are short.

Except *ūs*

   (*a*) in gen. sg., nom., voc. and acc. pl. of 4th
declension nouns, e.g. *gradūs*, *genūs*.

   (*b*) in the nom. sg. of consonant stem 3rd
declension nouns having gen. sg. with a
long penultimate syllable, e.g. *tellūs*
(-*ūris*), *palūs* (-*ūdis*), *virtūs* (-*ūtis*).

And except *īs*

   (*c*) in dat. and abl. pl., e.g. *mensīs*, *dominīs*,
vinīs.

   (*d*) in nom. and acc. pl. of 3rd declension -*i*
stems, e.g. *omnīs*, *navīs*.

   (*e*) in the 2nd pers. sg. of 4th conjugation
verbs, e.g. *audīs* ; and in *sīs*, and compounds of *sīs*, as *possīs* ; and in *velīs*,
nolīs, *malīs*, and *īs* (from *eo*).

E. Quantity of syllables determined by position in the same word.

1. A syllable ending with a vowel or diphthong, immediately followed by a syllable beginning with a vowel, or with *h* and a vowel, is short : e.g. *vĭa, prăeustus, trăhit.*

Except

(a) in the case of genitives in -*ius*, e.g. *alīus, solīus, utrīus.* (But note *illīus.*)

(b) *e* preceding *i* in 5th declension, e.g. *diĕi*, and in *ĕi* (from *is*).

(c) the syllable *fī* in *fīo.* (But note *fĭeri, fĭerem,* the *i* being short before *er.*

2. A syllable containing a vowel immediately followed by two consonants, or by *x* or *z*, which are really double consonants (*cs* and *ds*) is long ; e.g. *regent, auspex.*

Except

(a) if the two consonants are a combination of one of the following, *b, c, d, f, g, p, t,* with (following) *l* or *r.*

If a short vowel precedes such a combination the syllable is not necessarily long.

Finally it must be remembered that these rules apply to Latin words only, and not to the many Greek proper names which will be met with in this book.

Let us now see if, with the information given above, we can scan one of the hexameters of this poem.

Looking at the first line

Iam nitidum retegente diem noctisque fugante

(i) see first whether any syllable requires to be *elided*, i.e. not taken into account. (There is none ; elision is not very frequent in Ovid.)

(ii) mark long (–) all syllables whose long quantity can be determined by the rules given above.

Iam, dum, ent, em, noc, tis, ant

are all long syllables (by Rule E. 2), giving us now

Iām nitidūm retegēnte diēm nōctīsque fugānte

(iii) mark short all syllables whose short quantity can be determined by rule.

The final -*te* of *retegente,* *que,* and the final -*te* of *fugante* we know to be short (by Rule B. 2).

di is short (by Rule E. 1)

giving us

Iām nitidūm retegēntĕ dĭēm nōctīsquĕ fugāntĕ

Now work backwards from the end of the line, because the pattern of the last two feet (– ◡ ◡ | – – or – ◡) is constant. This gives us, for these feet

   5   6
| *tīsquĕ fŭ* | *gāntĕ*

Working backwards again, the fourth foot is obviously a spondee :

$$\overset{4}{\mid \bar{em} \; \bar{noc} \mid}$$

and the 3rd, a dactyl,

$$\overset{3}{\mid \bar{gen} \breve{te} \; \breve{di} \mid}$$

This leaves us with six syllables to be got into the first two feet, which must thus be dactyls.

$$\overset{1}{\bar{Iam} \; \breve{ni} \breve{ti}} \mid \overset{2}{\bar{dum} \; \breve{re} \breve{te}} \mid$$

And the whole line, divided into feet and with the quantities marked, is

$$\overset{1}{\bar{Iam} \; \breve{ni} \breve{ti}} \mid \overset{2}{\bar{dum} \; \breve{re} \breve{te}} \mid \overset{3}{\bar{gen} \breve{te} \; \breve{di}} \mid \overset{4}{\bar{em} \; \bar{noc}} \mid \overset{5}{\bar{tis} \breve{que} \; \breve{fu}} \mid \overset{6}{\bar{gan} \breve{te}}$$

One thing remains to be done before our scansion is complete. It is a rule that usually in the 3rd foot, more rarely in the 4th, one word must end and another begin. This is called the *caesura* or ' cutting '. If this break occurs after the first syllable of the foot the caesura is said to be *strong* ; if after the second, *weak*. In line 1 we obviously have a weak caesura in the 3rd foot. The caesura is regularly marked in scansion by a pair of vertical lines.

Thus the scansion of our line, as completed, is

$$\bar{I}am\ n\breve{i}t\breve{i} \mid d\bar{u}m\ r\bar{e}t\breve{e} \mid g\bar{e}nt\breve{e} \parallel d\breve{i} \mid \bar{e}m\ n\bar{o}c \mid t\bar{i}sq\breve{u}e\ f\breve{u} \mid g\bar{a}nt\breve{e}$$

You will find that, with careful attention to the pronunciation of Latin words, you will gradually learn to scan by ear, without the necessity of applying for help to the rules of prosody. You should try to develop this power as early as possible.

Note that the scheme of the hexameter makes it elastic and gives it a variable length, as long as 17 or as short as 13 syllables. This makes possible such lines as

$$qu\bar{a}dr\breve{u}p\breve{e} \mid d\bar{a}nt\breve{e}\ p\breve{u} \mid tr\bar{e}m\ s\breve{o}n\breve{i} \mid t\bar{u}\ qu\breve{a}t\breve{i}t \mid \bar{u}ng\breve{u}l\breve{a} \mid$$
$$c\bar{a}mp\breve{u}m$$

(where the poet, describing the galloping of horses, imitates the sound of them),

and as

$$\bar{i}ll(i)\ \bar{i}n \mid t\bar{e}r\ s\bar{e} \mid s\bar{e}\ m\bar{a}g \mid n\bar{a}\ v\bar{i} \mid br\bar{a}cch\breve{i}\breve{a} \mid t\bar{o}ll\bar{u}nt$$

(where again sound is matched to sense, for the line describes the alternate blows upon an anvil delivered by two smiths).

P. OVIDI NASONIS

METAMORPHOSEON

LIBER OCTAVUS

How Megara was besieged by King Minos of Crete
Iam nitidum retegente diem noctisque fugante
tempora Lucifero cadit Eurus, et umida surgunt
nubila : dant placidi cursum redeuntibus Austri
Aeacidis Cephaloque, quibus feliciter acti
ante exspectatum portus tenuere petitos.   5
interea Minos Lelegeïa litora vastat
praetemptatque sui vires Mavortis in urbe
Alcathoi, quam Nisus habet, cui splendidus ostro
inter honoratos medioque in vertice canos
crinis inhaerebat, magni fiducia regni.   10

Sexta resurgebant orientis cornua lunae,
et pendebat adhuc belli fortuna, diuque
inter utrumque volat dubiis Victoria pennis.
regia turris erat vocalibus addita muris,
in quibus auratam proles Letoïa fertur   15
deposuisse lyram : saxo sonus eius inhaesit.
saepe illuc solita est ascendere filia Nisi

et petere exiguo resonantia saxa lapillo,
tum cum pax esset ; bello quoque saepe solebat
spectare ex illa rigidi certamina Martis.   20
iamque mora belli procerum quoque nomina norat
armaque equosque habitusque Cydoneasque phare-
    tras.
noverat ante alios faciem ducis Europaei,
plus etiam quam nosse sat est.

How Scylla, daughter of Nisus, the Megarian King,
fell in love with Minos

                    hac iudice Minos,
seu caput abdiderat cristata casside pennis,   25
in galea formosus erat : seu sumpserat auro
fulgentem clipeum, clipeum sumpsisse decebat.
torserat adductis hastilia lenta lacertis :
laudabat virgo iunctam cum viribus artem.
imposito calamo patulos sinuaverat arcus :   30
sic Phoebum sumptis iurabat stare sagittis.
cum vero faciem dempto nudaverat aere,
purpureusque albi stratis insignia pictis
terga premebat equi spumantiaque ora regebat,
vix sua, vix sanae virgo Niseïa compos   35
mentis erat : felix iaculum, quod tangeret ille,
quaeque manu premeret, felicia frena vocabat.
impetus est illi, liceat modo, ferre per agmen
virgineos hostile gradus ; est impetus illi
turribus e summis in Gnosia mittere corpus   40

castra, vel aeratas hosti recludere portas,
vel siquid Minos aliud velit. utque sedebat
candida Dictaei spectans tentoria regis,
' laeter,' ait ' doleamne geri lacrimabile bellum,
in dubio est : doleo, quod Minos hostis amanti est ; 45
sed nisi bella forent, numquam mihi cognitus esset.
me tamen accepta poterat deponere bellum
obside : me comitem, me pacis pignus haberet.
si quae te genuit, talis, pulcherrime rerum,
qualis es ipse, fuit, merito deus arsit in illa.   50
o ego ter felix, si pennis lapsa per auras
Gnosiaci possem castris insistere regis,
fassaque me flammasque meas, qua dote, rogarem,
vellet emi : tantum patrias ne posceret arces.
nam pereant potius sperata cubilia, quam sim   55
proditione potens. quamvis saepe utile vinci
victoris placidi fecit clementia multis.
iusta gerit certe pro nato bella perempto,
et causaque valet causamque tuentibus armis.
ut puto, vincemur. qui si manet exitus urbem,   60
cur suus haec illi reseret mea moenia Mavors
et non noster amor? melius sine caede moraque
impensaque sui poterit superare cruoris.
non metuam certe, ne quis tua pectora, Minos,
vulneret imprudens. quis enim tam durus, ut in
      te   65
derigere immitem non inscius audeat hastam? '

How Scylla, for love of Minos, betrayed her father to him

coepta placent et stat sententia tradere secum
dotalem patriam finemque imponere bello.
verum velle parum est. ' aditus custodia servat,
claustraque portarum genitor tenet. hunc ego solum
infelix timeo, solus mea vota moratur.   71
di facerent, sine patre forem! sibi quisque profecto
est deus : ignavis precibus Fortuna repugnat.
altera iamdudum succensa cupidine tanto
perdere gauderet quodcumque obstaret amori.   75
et cur ulla foret me fortior? ire per ignes
et gladios ausim. nec in hoc tamen ignibus ullis
aut gladiis opus est : opus est mihi crine paterno.
illa mihi est auro pretiosior, illa beatam
purpura me votique mei factura potentem.'   80

    Talia dicenti curarum maxima nutrix
nox intervenit, tenebrisque audacia crevit.
prima quies aderat, qua curis fessa diurnis
pectora somnus habet. thalamos taciturna paternos
intrat et, heu facinus, fatali nata parentem   85
crine suum spoliat, praedaque potita nefanda
per medios hostes (meriti fiducia tanta est)   88
pervenit ad regem. quem sic adfata paventem est :
' suasit amor facinus. proles ego regia Nisi   90
Scylla tibi trado patriaeque meosque penates.
praemia nulla peto, nisi te. cape pignus amoris
purpureum crinem, nec me nunc tradere crinem,

sed patrium tibi crede caput,' scelerataque dextra
munera porrexit.

*How Scylla, scorned by Minos for her treachery, plunged
    into the sea to follow his departing fleet and was changed
    into the sea-bird Ciris*

      Minos porrecta refugit :   95
turbatusque novi respondit imagine facti :
' Di te summoveant, o nostri infamia saecli,
orbe suo, tellusque tibi pontusque negetur.
certe ego non patiar Iovis incunabula, Creten,
qui meus est orbis, tantum contingere monstrum.' 100
dixit : et ut leges captis iustissimus auctor
hostibus imposuit, classis retinacula solvi
iussit et aeratas impleri remige puppes.
Scylla freto postquam deductas nare carinas,
nec praestare ducem sceleris sibi praemia vidit, 105
consumptis precibus violentam transit in iram
intendensque manus, passis furibunda capillis,
' quo fugis,' exclamat ' meritorum auctore relicta,
o patriae praelate meae, praelate parenti?
quo fugis, immitis, cuius victoria nostrum 110
et scelus et meritum est? nec te data munera, nec te
noster amor movit, nec quod spes omnis in unum
te mea congesta est? nam quo deserta revertar?
in patriam? superata iacet. sed finge manere :
proditione mea clausa est mihi. patris ad ora, 115
quem tibi donavi? cives odere merentem :

finitimi exemplum metuunt. exponimur orbe
terrarum, nobis ut Crete sola pateret.
hanc quoque si prohibes, et nos, ingrate, relinquis,
non genetrix Europa tibi est, sed inhospita Syrtis, 120
Armeniae tigres austroque agitata Charybdis.
nec Iove tu natus, nec mater imagine tauri
ducta tua est : generis falsa est ea fabula : verus,
et ferus et captus nullius amore iuvencae,
qui te progenuit, taurus fuit. exige poenas, 125
Nise pater! gaudete malis, modo prodita, nostris
moenia! nam fateor, merui et sum digna perire.
sed tamen ex illis aliquis, quos impia laesi,
me perimat. cur, qui vicisti crimine nostro,
insequeris crimen? scelus hoc patriaeque patrique, 130
officium tibi sit.... ecquid ad aures
perveniunt mea dicta tuas? an inania venti 134
verba ferunt idemque tuas, ingrate, carinas? 135
me miseram! properare iuvat, divulsaque remis 138
unda sonat. mecumque simul mea terra recedit.
nil agis, o frustra meritorum oblite meorum : 140
insequar invitum, puppimque amplexa recurvam
per freta longa trahar.' vix dixerat, insilit undis
consequiturque rates, faciente cupidine vires,
Gnosiacaeque haeret comes invidiosa carinae.
quam pater ut vidit (nam iam pendebat in auras 145
et modo factus erat fulvis haliaeëtos alis),
ibat, ut haerentem rostro laceraret adunco.

illa metu puppim dimisit, et aura cadentem
sustinuisse levis, ne tangeret aequora, visa est.
pluma fuit : plumis in avem mutata vocatur   150
ciris, et a tonso est hoc nomen adepta capillo.

How Daedalus, the great craftsman, built for Minos
the Labyrinth, to house the half-beast Minotaur

Vota Iovi Minos, taurorum corpora centum,
solvit, ut egressus ratibus Curetida terram
contigit, et spoliis decorata est regia fixis.
creverat opprobrium generis, foedumque patebat. 155
destinat hunc Minos thalamis removere pudorem, 157
multiplicique domo caecisque includere tectis.
Daedalus ingenio fabrae celeberrimus artis
ponit opus ; turbatque notas, et lumina flexum   160
ducit in errorem variarum ambage viarum.
non secus ac liquidus Phrygiis Maeandrus in arvis
ludit et ambiguo lapsu refluitque fluitque,
occurrensque sibi venturas aspicit undas,
et nunc ad fontes, nunc ad mare versus apertum   165
incertas exercet aquas : ita Daedalus implet
innumeras errore vias, vixque ipse reverti
ad limen potuit : tanta est fallacia tecti.

How Ariadne, daughter of Minos, fleeing from Crete after
aiding Theseus to slay the Minotaur, had her diadem
changed into a constellation by Bacchus.

quo postquam geminam tauri iuvenisque figuram
clausit, et Actaeo bis pastum sanguine monstrum 170

'COMITEMQUE SUAM CRUDELIS IN ILLO LITORE
DESTITUIT'

tertia sors annis domuit repetita novenis,
utque ope virginea nullis iterata priorum
ianua difficilis filo est inventa relecto :
protinus Aegides rapta Minoide Diam
vela dedit, comitemque suam crudelis in illo   175
litore destituit.   desertae et multa querenti
amplexus et opem Liber tulit, utque perenn·
sidere clara foret, sumptam de fronte coronam
immisit caelo.   tenues volat illa per auras,
dumque volat, gemmae nitidos vertuntur in
     ignes   180

consistuntque loco, specie remanente coronae,
qui medius Nixique genu est, Anguemque tenentis.

*How Daedalus, wearying of his long exile in Crete, sought
to escape to Athens, with his son Icarus, by flying
through the air on man-made wings*

Daedalus interea Creten longumque perosus
exilium tactusque loci natalis amore,
clausus erat pelago. ' Terras licet ' inquit ' et undas
obstruat, at caelum certe patet. ibimus illac.   186
omnia possideat, non possidet aëra Minos.'
dixit et ignotas animum dimittit in artes
naturamque novat. nam ponit in ordine pennas,
a minima coeptas, longam breviore sequenti,   190
ut clivo crevisse putes : sic rustica quondam
fistula disparibus paulatim surgit avenis.
tum lino medias et ceris alligat imas,
atque ita compositas parvo curvamine flectit,
ut veras imitetur aves. puer Icarus una   195
stabat et, ignarus sua se tractare pericla,
ore renidenti modo, quas vaga moverat aura,
captabat plumas, flavam modo pollice ceram
mollibat, lusuque suo mirabile patris
impediebat opus. postquam manus ultima coeptis
imposita est, geminas opifex libravit in alas   201
ipse suum corpus motaque pependit in aura.
instruit et natum, ' medio ' que ' ut limite curras,
Icare,' ait ' moneo, ne, si demissior ibis,

c

unda gravet pennas, si celsior, ignis adurat :   205
inter utrumque vola. nec te spectare Booten
aut Helicen iubeo strictumque Orionis ensem :
me duce carpe viam.' pariter praecepta volandi
tradit et ignotas umeris accommodat alas.
inter opus monitusque genae maduere seniles,   210
et patriae tremuere manus. dedit oscula nato
non iterum repetenda suo, pennisque levatus
ante volat, comitique timet, velut ales, ab alto
quae teneram prolem produxit in aëra nido ;
hortaturque sequi, damnosasque erudit artes   215
et movet ipse suas et nati respicit alas.
hos aliquis, tremula dum captat harundine pisces,
aut pastor baculo stivave innixus arator
vidit et obstipuit, quique aethera carpere possent,
credidit esse deos.

How Icarus, flying too near the sun, lost his wings and fell
to his death in the sea

                et iam Iunonia laeva   220
parte Samos (fuerant Delosque Parosque relictae),
dextra Lebinthus erat fecundaque melle Calymne,
cum puer audaci coepit gaudere volatu,
deseruitque ducem caelique cupidine tractus
altius egit iter. rapidi vicinia solis   225
mollit odoratas, pennarum vincula, ceras.
tabuerant cerae : nudos quatit ille lacertos
remigioque carens non ullas percipit auras,

'PONIT IN ORDINE PENNAS

oraque caerulea patrium clamantia nomen
excipiuntur aqua : quae nomen traxit ab illo.   230
at pater infelix, nec iam pater, ' Icare,' dixit,
' Icare,' dixit ' ubi es? qua te regione requiram? '
' Icare ' dicebat : pennas aspexit in undis,
devovitque suas artes, corpusque sepulchro
condidit, et tellus a nomine dicta sepulti.   235

How the nephew of Daedalus, Perdix, who, having been flung
by him from the Acropolis, was changed by Minerva
into a partridge, rejoiced in the sorrow of Daedalus

Hunc miseri tumulo ponentem corpora nati
garrula limoso prospexit ab elice perdix,
et plausit pennis testataque gaudia cantu est :
unica tunc volucris, nec visa prioribus annis,
factaque nuper avis, longum tibi, Daedale, crimen.
namque huic tradiderat, fatorum ignara, docendam
progeniem germana suam, natalibus actis   242
bis puerum senis, animi ad praecepta capacis.
ille etiam medio spinas in pisce notatas
traxit in exemplum ferroque incidit acuto   245
perpetuos dentes et serrae repperit usum.
primus et ex uno duo ferrea bracchia nodo
vinxit, ut aequali spatio distantibus illis
altera pars staret, pars altera duceret orbem.
Daedalus invidit, sacraque ex arce Minervae   250
praecipitem misit, lapsum mentitus. at illum,
quae favet ingeniis, excepit Pallas, avemque

reddidit, et medio velavit in aëre pennis.
sed vigor ingenii quondam velocis in alas
inque pedes abiit : nomen, quod et ante, remansit. 255
non tamen haec alte volucris sua corpora tollit,
nec facit in ramis altoque cacumine nidos :
propter humum volitat ponitque in saepibus ova
antiquique memor metuit sublimia casus.

How Theseus, returning home from Crete, was begged by the
townsfolk of Calydon to aid them in destroying a mon-
strous boar, sent by Diana to ravage their land

Iamque fatigatum tellus Aetnaea tenebat   260
Daedalon, et sumptis pro supplice Cocalus armis
mitis habebatur ; iam lamentabile Athenae
pendere desierant Thesea laude tributum.
templa coronantur, bellatricemque Minervam
cum Iove disque vocant aliis, quos sanguine voto 265
muneribusque datis et acerris turis adorant.
sparserat Argolicas nomen vaga fama per urbes
Theseos, et populi, quos dives Achaia cepit,
huius opem magnis imploravere periclis.
huius opem Calydon, quamvis Meleagron haberet,
sollicita supplex petiit prece.   causa petendi   271
sus erat, infestae famulus vindexque Dianae.
Oenea namque ferunt pleni successibus anni
primitias frugum Cereri, sua vina Lyaeo,
Palladios flavae latices libasse Minervae.   275
coeptus ab agricolis superos pervenit ad omnes

ambitiosus honor : solas sine ture relictas
praeteritae cessasse ferunt Latoidos aras.
tangit et ira deos. ' at non impune feremus,
quaeque inhonoratae, non et dicemur inultae '   280
inquit, et Oeneos ultorem spreta per agros
misit aprum, quanto maiores herbida tauros
non habet Epiros, sed habent Sicula arva minores.
sanguine et igne micant oculi, riget ardua cervix,
et saetae similes rigidis hastilibus horrent :   285
fervida cum rauco latos stridore per armos   287
spuma fluit, dentes aequantur dentibus Indis,
fulmen ab ore venit, frondes adflatibus ardent.
is modo crescentes segetes proculcat in herba,   290
nunc matura metit fleturi vota coloni
et Cererem in spicis intercipit : area frustra
et frustra exspectant promissas horrea messes.
sternuntur gravidi longo cum palmite fetus
bacaque cum ramis semper frondentis olivae.   295
saevit et in pecudes : non has pastorve canesve,
non armenta truces possunt defendere tauri.
diffugiunt populi, nec se nisi moenibus urbis
esse putant tutos : donec Meleagros et una
lecta manus iuvenum coiere cupidine laudis :   300

How many great hunters—and one huntress—joined
Prince Meleager to hunt the Calydonian boar

Tyndaridae gemini, spectatus caestibus alter,
alter equo, primaeque ratis molitor Iason,

et cum Pirithoo, felix concordia, Theseus,
et duo Thestiadae et, proles Aphareïa, Lynceus
et velox Idas et iam non femina Caeneus, 305
Leucippusque ferox iaculoque insignis Acastus,
Hippothousque Dryasque et cretus Amyntore
    Phoenix,
Actoridaeque pares, et missus ab Elide Phyleus.
nec Telamon aberat magnique creator Achillis,
cumque Pheretiade et Hyanteo Iolao 310
impiger Eurytion et cursu invictus Echion,
Naryciusque Lelex Panopeusque Hyleusque feroxque
Hippasus, et primis etiamnum Nestor in annis,
et quos Hippocoon antiquis misit Amyclis,
Penelopesque socer cum Parrhasio Ancaeo, 315
Ampycidesque sagax et adhuc a coniuge tutus
Oeclides, nemorisque decus Tegeaea Lycaei.
rasilis huic summam mordebat fibula vestem,
crinis erat simplex, nodum collectus in unum :
ex umero pendens resonabat eburnea laevo 320
telorum custos, arcum quoque laeva tenebat.
talis erat cultu : facies, quam dicere vere
virgineam in puero, puerilem in virgine posses.
hanc pariter vidit, pariter Calydonius heros
optavit, renuente deo, flammasque latentes 325
hausit, et ' o felix, siquem dignabitur ' inquit
' ista virum! ' nec plura sinit tempusque pudorque
dicere : maius opus magni certaminis urguet.

*How the hunt began, and how Enaesimus was slain
by the boar's tusks*

Silva frequens trabibus, quam nulla ceciderat aetas
incipit a plano devexaque prospicit arva.   330
quo postquam venere viri, pars retia tendunt,
vincula pars adimunt canibus, pars pressa sequuntur
signa pedum, cupiuntque suum reperire periclum.   '
concava vallis erat, quo se demittere rivi
adsuerant pluvialis aquae : tenet ima lacunae   335
lenta salix ulvaeque leves iuncique palustres
viminaque et longa parvae sub harundine cannae.
hinc aper excitus medios violentus in hostes
fertur, ut excussis elisi nubibus ignes.
sternitur incursu nemus, et propulsa fragorem   340
silva dat.   exclamant iuvenes, praetentaque forti
tela tenent dextra lato vibrantia ferro.
ille ruit spargitque canes, ut quisque furenti
obstat, et obliquo latrantes dissipat ictu.
cuspis Echionio primum contorta lacerto   345
vana fuit, truncoque dedit leve vulnus acerno.
proxima, si nimiis mittentis viribus usa
non foret, in tergo visa est haesura petito :
longius it.   auctor teli Pagasaeus Iason.
' Phoebe,' ait Ampycides,' si te coluique coloque,   350
da mihi quod petitur certo contingere telo! '
qua potuit, precibus deus adnuit : ictus ab illo
    est,

sed sine vulnere, aper : ferrum Diana volanti
abstulerat iaculo ; lignum sine acumine venit.
ira feri mota est, nec fulmine lenius arsit : 355

HUNTING THE BOAR

emicat ex oculis, spirat quoque pectore flamma.
utque volat moles adducto concita nervo,
cum petit aut muros aut plenas milite turres,
in iuvenes certo sic impete vulnificus sus
fertur et Eupalamon Pelagonaque, dextra tuentes

cornua, prosternit : socii rapuere iacentes.　　**361**
at non letiferos effugit Enaesimus ictus
Hippocoonte satus : trepidantem et terga parantem
vertere succiso liquerunt poplite nervi.

*How the boar was first wounded by Atalanta, and
how Ancaeus was slain*

forsitan et Pyiius citra Troiana perisset　　**365**
tempora : sed sumpto posita conamine ab hasta
arboris insiluit, quae stabat proxima, ramis
despexitque, loco tutus, quem fugerat hostem.
dentibus ille ferox in querno stipite tritis
imminet exitio fidensque recentibus armis　　**370**
Eurytidae magni rostro femur hausit adunco.
at gemini, nondum caelestia sidera, fratres,
ambo conspicui, nive candidioribus ambo
vectabantur equis, ambo vibrata per auras
hastarum tremulo quatiebant spicula motu.　　**375**
vulnera fecissent, nisi saetiger inter opacas
nec iaculis isset nec equo loca pervia, silvas.
persequitur Telamon, studioque incautus eundi
pronus ab arborea cecidit radice retentus.
dum levat hunc Peleus, celerem Tegeaea sagittam **380**
imposuit nervo sinuatoque expulit arcu.
fixa sub aure feri summum destringit harundo
corpus, et exiguo rubefecit sanguine saetas.
nec tamen illa sui successu laetior ictus,
quam Meleagros erat. primus vidisse putatur,　　**385**

et primus sociis visum ostendisse cruorem,
et ' meritum ' dixisse ' feres virtutis honorem.'
erubuere viri, seque exhortantur et addunt
cum clamore animos, iaciuntque sine ordine tela.
turba nocet iactis et, quos petit, impedit ictus.   390
ecce furens contra sua fata bipennifer Arcas
' discite, femineis quid tela virilia praestent,
o iuvenes, operique meo concedite! ' dixit.
' ipsa suis licet hunc Latonia protegat armis,
invita tamen hunc perimet mea dextra Diana.'   395
talia magniloquo tumidus memoraverat ore
ancipitemque manu tollens utraque securim
institerat digitis, pronos suspensus in ictus :
occupat audentem, quaque est via proxima leto,
summa ferus geminos direxit ad inguina dentes.   400
concidit Ancaeus, glomerataque sanguine multo
viscera lapsa fluunt : madefacta est terra cruore.

How the boar was slain at last by Meleager

ibat in adversum proles Ixionis hostem
Pirithous valida quatiens venabula dextra.
cui ' procul ' Aegides ' o me mihi carior ' inquit   405
' pars animae consiste meae! licet eminus esse
fortibus : Ancaeo nocuit temeraria virtus.'
dixit et aerata torsit grave cuspide cornum.
quo bene librato votique potente futuro
obstitit aesculea frondosus ab arbore ramus.   410
misit et Aesonides iaculum, quod casus ab illo

vertit in immeriti fatum latrantis, et inter
ilia coniectum tellure per ilia fixum est.
at manus Oenidae variat, missisque duabus
hasta prior terra, medio stetit altera tergo.   **415**
nec mora : dum saevit, dum corpora versat in orbem
stridentemque novo spumam cum sanguine fundit,
vulneris auctor adest, hostemque inritat ad iram
splendidaque adversos venabula condit in armos.
gaudia testantur socii clamore secundo   **420**
victricemque petunt dextrae coniungere dextram ;
immanemque ferum multa tellure iacentem
mirantes spectant, neque adhuc contingere tutum
esse putant, sed tela tamen sua quisque cruentat.

How Meleager slew his uncles, Plexippus and Toxeus, for
having resented his bestowal of the spoils upon Atalanta

ipse pede imposito caput exitiabile pressit   **425**
atque ita ' sume mei spolium, Nonacria, iuris,'
dixit ' et in partem veniat mea gloria tecum.'
protinus exuvias, rigidis horrentia saetis
terga dat et magnis insignia dentibus ora.
illi laetitiae est cum munere muneris auctor.   **430**
invidere alii, totoque erat agmine murmur.
e quibus ingenti tendentes bracchia voce
' pone age nec titulos intercipe, femina, nostros,'
Thestiadae clamant, ' nec te fiducia formae
decipiat, ne sit longe tibi captus amore   **435**
auctor,' et huic adimunt munus, ius muneris illi.

non tulit, et tumida frendens Mavortius ira
' discite, raptores alieni ' dixit ' honoris,
facta minis quantum distent,' hausitque nefando
pectora Plexippi nil tale timentia ferro.   440
Toxea, quid faciat, dubium pariterque volentem
ulcisci fratrem fraternaque fata timentem
haud patitur dubitare diu, calidumque prioris
caede recalfecit consorti sanguine telum.

How Althaea, mother of Meleager, long torn by her two
*   loyalties, at last revenged herself upon him for his slaying*
*   of her brothers by committing to the flames the sacred*
*   brand on which his life depended*

Dona deum templis nato victore ferebat,   445
cum videt exstinctos fratres Althaea referri.
quae plangore dato maestis clamoribus urbem
implet, et auratis mutavit vestibus atras.
at simul est auctor necis editus, excidit omnis
luctus : et a lacrimis in poenae versus amorem
       est.   450
stipes erat, quem, cum partus enixa iaceret
Thestias, in flammam triplices posuere sorores,
staminaque impresso fatalia pollice nentes
' tempora ' dixerunt ' eadem lignoque tibique,
o modo nate, damus.' quo postquam carmine dicto
excessere deae, flagrantem mater ab igne   456
eripuit torrem sparsitque liquentibus undis.
ille diu fuerat penetralibus abditus imis,

servatusque tuos, iuvenis, servaverat annos.
protulit hunc genetrix, taedasque et fragmina poni
imperat, et positis inimicos admovet ignes.   461
tum conata quater flammis imponere ramum,
coepta quater tenuit.   pugnant materque sororque,
et diversa trahunt unum duo nomina pectus.
saepe metu sceleris pallebant ora futuri,   465
saepe suum fervens oculis dabat ira ruborem,
et modo nescio quid similis crudele minanti
vultus erat, modo quem misereri credere posses.
cumque ferus lacrimas animi siccaverat ardor,
inveniebantur lacrimae tamen.   utque carina,   470
quam ventus ventoque rapit contrarius aestus,
vim geminam sentit, paretque incerta duobus,
Thestias haud aliter dubiis adfectibus errat
perque vices ponit positamque resuscitat iram.
incipit esse tamen melior germana parente,   475
et, consanguineas ut sanguine leniat umbras,
impietate pia est.   nam postquam pestifer ignis
convaluit, ' rogus iste cremet mea viscera ' dixit.
utque manu dira lignum fatale tenebat,
ante sepulchrales infelix astitit aras   480
' poenarum ' que ' deae triplices, furialibus,' inquit,
' Eumenides, sacris vultus advertite vestros.
ulciscor facioque nefas.   mors morte pianda est :
in scelus addendum scelus est, in funera funus :
per coacervatos pereat domus impia luctus.   485

an felix Oeneus nato victore fruetur,
Thestius orbus erit? melius lugebitis ambo.
vos modo, fraterni manes animaeque recentes,
officium sentite meum, magnoque paratas
accipite inferias, uteri mala pignora nostri.   490
ei mihi! quo rapior? fratres ignoscite matri!
deficiunt ad coepta manus. meruisse fatemur
illum, cur pereat : mortis mihi displicet auctor.
ergo impune feret, vivusque et victor et ipso
successu tumidus regnum Calydonis habebit,   495
vos cinis exiguus gelidaeque iacebitis umbrae?
haud equidem patiar. pereat sceleratus, et ille
spemque patris regnumque trahat patriaeque ruinam.
mens ubi materna est? ubi sunt pia iura parentum
et quos sustinui bis mensum quinque labores?   500
o utinam primis arsisses ignibus infans,
idque ego passa forem! vixisti munere nostro ;
nunc merito moriere tuo. cape praemia facti,
bisque datam, primum partu, mox stipite rapto,
redde animam, vel me fraternis adde sepulchris. 505
et cupio et nequeo. quid agam? modo vulnera fratrum
ante oculos mihi sunt et tantae caedis imago,
nunc animum pietas maternaque nomina frangunt.
me miseram! male vincetis, sed vincite, fratres,
dummodo quae dedero vobis solacia, vosque   510
ipsa sequar.' dixit, dextraque aversa trementi
funereum torrem medios coniecit in ignes.

aut dedit, aut visus gemitus est ille dedisse
stipes, ut invitis correptus ab ignibus arsit.

How Meleager died, and how his sisters, grieving for his
death, were changed by Diana into guinea-hens

inscius atque absens flamma Meleagros ab illa   515
uritur, et caecis torreri viscera sentit
ignibus, ac magnos superat virtute dolores.
quod tamen ignavo cadat et sine sanguine leto,
maeret, et Ancaei felicia vulnera dicit :
grandaevumque patrem fratresque piasque sorores
cum gemitu sociamque tori vocat ore supremo,   521
forsitan et matrem.   crescunt ignisque dolorque,
languescuntque iterum : simul est exstinctus uterque,
inque leves abiit paulatim spiritus auras
paulatim cana prunam velante favilla.   525

    Alta iacet Calydon : lugent iuvenesque senesque,
vulgusque proceresque gemunt, scissaeque capillos
planguntur matres Calydonides Eveninae.
pulvere canitiem genitor vultusque seniles
foedat humi fusus, spatiosumque increpat aevum. 530
nam de matre manus diri sibi conscia facti
exegit poenas acto per viscera ferro.
non mihi si centum deus ora sonantia linguis
ingeniumque capax totumque Helicona dedisset,
tristia persequerer miserarum dicta sororum.   535
immemores decoris liventia pectora tundunt,
dumque manet corpus, corpus refoventque foventque

DIANA

D

oscula dant ipsi, posito dant oscula lecto.
post cinerem cineres haustos ad pectora pressant,
adfusaeque iacent tumulo signataque saxo 540
nomina complexae lacrimas in nomina fundunt.
quas Parthaoniae tandem Latonia clade
exsatiata domus praeter Gorgenque nurumque
nobilis Alcmenae natis in corpore pennis
adlevat et longas per bracchia porrigit alas 545
corneaque ora facit versasque per aëra mittit.

Achelous, the river-god, feasting Theseus on his homeward way,
tells how certain nymphs were changed into islands

Interea Theseus sociati parte laboris
functus Erechtheas Tritonidos ibat ad arces.
clausit iter fecitque moras Achelous eunti
imbre tumens. ' succede meis,' ait ' inclite, tectis, 550
Cecropida, nec te committe rapacibus undis.
terre trabes solidas obliquaque volvere magno
murmure saxa solent. vidi contermina ripae
cum gregibus stabula alta trahi ; nec fortibus illic
profuit armentis, nec equis velocibus esse. 555
multa quoque hic torrens nivibus de monte solutis
corpora turbineo iuvenalia vertice mersit.
tutior est requies, solito dum flumina currant
limite, dum tenues capiat suus alveus undas.'
adnuit Aegides, ' utar,' que ' Acheloe, domoque 560
consilioque tuo ' respondit, et usus utroque est.
pumice multicavo nec levibus atria tophis

structa subit : molli tellus erat umida musco ;
summa lacunabant alterno murice conchae.
iamque duas lucis partes Hyperione menso   565
discubuere toris Theseus comitesque laborum :
hac Ixionides, illa Troezenius heros
parte Lelex, raris iam sparsus tempora canis,
quosque alios parili fuerat dignatus honore
amnis Acarnanum, laetissimus hospite tanto.   570
protinus adpositas nudae vestigia nymphae
instruxere epulis mensas, dapibusque remotis
in gemma posuere merum.   tum maximus heros,
aequora prospiciens oculis subiecta, ' quis ' inquit
' ille locus? ' digitoque ostendit, et ' insula nomen 575
quod gerit illa, doce :   quamquam non una videtur.'
amnis ad haec ' non est ' inquit ' quod cernitis, unum.
quinque iacent terrae :   spatium discrimina fallit.
quoque minus spretae factum mirere Dianae,
Naides hae fuerant, quae cum bis quinque iuvencos
mactassent rurisque deos ad sacra vocassent,   581
immemores nostri festas duxere choreas.
intumui, quantusque feror, cum plurimus unquam,
tantus eram, pariterque animis immanis et undis
a silvis silvas et ab arvis arva revulsi,   585
cumque loco nymphas, memores tum denique nostri,
in freta provolvi.   fluctus nosterque marisque
continuam diduxit humum, partesque resolvit
in totidem, mediis quot cernis Echinadas undis.'

28 OVID

ut tamen ipse vides, procul, en procul una recessit 590
insula, grata mihi ; Perimelen navita dicit :
huic ego virgineum dilectae nomen ademi ;
quod pater Hippodamas aegre tulit, inque profundum
propulit e scopulo periturae corpora natae.
excepi, nantemque ferens ' o proxima mundi 595
regna vagae,' dixi, ' sortite, Tridentifer, undae,
adfer opem, mersaeque, precor, feritate paterna 601
da, Neptune, locum ; vel sit locus ipsa licebit! '
dum loquor, amplexa est artus nova terra natantes,
et gravis increvit mutatis insula membris.' 610

*Lelex tells the scoffer Pirithous how an old peasant Philemon
and his wife Baucis entertained Jupiter and Mercury
unawares*

Amnis ab his tacuit. factum mirabile cunctos
moverat. inridet credentes, utque deorum
spretor erat mentisque ferox, Ixione natus
' ficta refers nimiumque putas, Acheloe, potentes
esse deos,' dixit ' si dant adimuntque figuras.' 615
obstipuere omnes, nec talia dicta probarunt ;
ante omnesque Lelex, animo maturus et aevo,
sic ait : ' immensa est finemque potentia caeli
non habet, et quicquid superi voluere, peractum est.
quoque minus dubites, tiliae contermina quercus 620
collibus est Phrygiis, modico circumdata muro :
ipse locum vidi ; nam me Pelopeïa Pittheus
misit in arva, suo quondam regnata parenti.

haud procul hinc stagnum est, tellus habitabilis olim,
nunc celebres mergis fulicisque palustribus undae. 625
Iuppiter huc specie mortali, cumque parente
venit Atlantiades positis caducifer alis.

'Venit Atlantiades ... caducifer'

mille domos adiere locum requiemque petentes :
mille domos clausere serae.   tamen una recepit,
parva quidem, stipulis et canna tecta palustri : 630
sed pia Baucis anus parilique aetate Philemon
illa sunt annis iuncti iuvenalibus, illa
consenuere casa paupertatemque fatendo
effecere levem nec iniqua mente ferendo.

nec refert, dominos illic, famulosne requiras :   635
tota domus duo sunt, idem parentque iubentque.

' Ergo ubi caelicolae parvos tetigere penates
summissoque humiles intrarunt vertice postes,
membra senex posito iussit relevare sedili,
quo superiniecit textum rude sedula Baucis.   640
inque foco tepidum cinerem dimovit et ignes
suscitat hesternos foliisque et cortice sicco
nutrit et ad flammas anima producit anili,
multifidasque faces ramaliaque arida tecto
detulit et minuit, parvoque admovit aëno.   645
quodque suus coniunx riguo collegerat horto,
truncat holus foliis.   furca levat ille bicorni
sordida terga suis nigro pendentia tigno,
servatoque diu resecat de tergore partem
exiguam, sectamque domat ferventibus undis.   650

' Interea medias fallunt sermonibus horas
concutiuntque torum de molli fluminis ulva   655
impositum lecto, sponda pedibusque salignis.
vestibus hunc velant, quas non nisi tempore festo
sternere consuerant : sed et haec vilisque vetusque
vestis erat, lecto non indignanda saligno.
accubuere dei.   mensam succincta tremensque   660
ponit anus.   mensae sed erat pes tertius impar :
testa parem fecit.   quae postquam subdita clivum
sustulit, aequatam mentae tersere virentes.
ponitur hic bicolor sincerae baca Minervae,

conditaque in liquida corna autumnalia faece,   665
intibaque et radix et lactis massa coacti,
ovaque non acri leviter versata favilla,
omnia fictilibus. post haec caelatus eodem
sistitur argento crater fabricataque fago
pocula, qua cava sunt, flaventibus inlita ceris.   670
parva mora est, epulasque foci misere calentes,
nec longae rursus referuntur vina senectae,
dantque locum mensis paulum seducta secundis.
hic nux, hic mixta est rugosis carica palmis
prunaque et in patulis redolentia mala canistris   675
et de purpureis collectae vitibus uvae.
candidus in medio favus est. super omnia vultus
accessere boni nec iners pauperque voluntas.

*How Philemon and Baucis, at last recognizing their guests,
were made guardians of their temple and were changed in
extreme old age into trees*

' Interea totiens haustum cratera repleri
sponte sua, per seque vident succrescere vina :   680
attoniti novitate pavent, manibusque supinis
concipiunt Baucisque preces timidusque Philemon
et veniam dapibus nullisque paratibus orant.
unicus anser erat, minimae custodia villae :
quem dis hospitibus domini mactare parabant.   685
ille celer penna tardos aetate fatigat
eluditque diu tandemque est visus ad ipsos
confugisse deos. superi vetuere necari,

" di " que " sumus, meritasque luet vicinia poenas
impia " dixerunt ; " vobis immunibus huius   690
esse mali dabitur. modo vestra relinquite tecta
ac nostros comitate gradus et in ardua montis
ite simul." parent ambo, baculisque levati
nituntur longo vestigia ponere clivo.

   ' Tantum aberant summo, quantum semel ire
      sagitta   695
missa potest : flexere oculos, et mersa palude
cetera prospiciunt, tantum sua tecta manere.
dumque ea mirantur, dum deflent fata suorum,
illa vetus, dominis etiam casa parva duobus,
vertitur in templum : furcas subiere columnae,   700
stramina flavescunt aurataque tecta videntur,
caelataeque fores, adopertaque marmore tellus.
talia tum placido Saturnius edidit ore :
" dicite, iuste senex et femina coniuge iusto
digna, quid optetis." cum Baucide pauca locutus
iudicium superis aperit commune Philemon :   ·   706
" esse sacerdotes delubraque vestra tueri
poscimus, et quoniam concordes egimus annos,
auferat hora duos eadem, nec coniugis umquam
busta meae videam, neu sim tumulandus ab illa."

   ' Vota fides sequitur : templi tutela fuere,   711
donec vita data est. annis aevoque soluti
ante gradus sacros cum starent forte locique
narrarent casus, frondere Philemona Baucis,

Baucida conspexit senior frondere Philemon.   715
iamque super geminos crescente cacumine vultus
mutua, dum licuit, reddebant dicta " vale " que
" o coniunx " dixere simul, simul abdita texit
ora frutex. ostendit adhuc Thyneïus illic
incola de gemino vicinos corpore truncos.   720
    ' Haec mihi non vani, (neque erat cur fallere vellent)
narravere senes. equidem pendentia vidi
serta super ramos, ponensque recentia dixi
" cura pii dis sunt, et qui coluere, coluntur." '

Achelous tells how Erysichthon the impious felled a holy tree in which dwelt a Dryad

    Desierat, cunctosque et res et moverat auctor, 725
Thesea praecipue. quem facta audire volentem
mira deum, innixus cubito Calydonius amnis
talibus adloquitur : ' sunt, o fortissime, quorum
forma semel mota est, et in hoc renovamine mansit ;
sunt, quibus in plures ius est transire figuras,   730
ut tibi, complexi terram maris incola, Proteu.
nam modo te iuvenem, modo te videre leonem ;
nunc violentus aper, nunc, quem tetigisse timerent,
anguis eras ; modo te faciebant cornua taurum.
saepe lapis poteras, arbor quoque saepe videri : 735
interdum, faciem liquidarum imitatus aquarum,
flumen eras, interdum undis contrarius ignis.
nec minus Autolyci coniunx, Erysichthone nata,
iuris habet. pater huius erat, qui numina divum

sperneret et nullos aris adoleret honores.   740
ille etiam Cereale nemus violasse securi
dicitur et lucos ferro temerasse vetustos.
stabat in his ingens annoso robore quercus,
una nemus : vittae mediam memoresque tabellae
sertaque cingebant, voti argumenta potentis.   745
saepe sub hac Dryades festas duxere choreas ;
saepe etiam manibus nexis ex ordine trunci
circuiere modum, mensuraque roboris ulnas
quinque ter implebat.   nec non et cetera tanto
silva sub hac, silva quanto fuit herba sub omni.   750
    ' Non tamen idcirco ferrum Triopeïus illa
abstinuit, famulosque iubet succidere sacrum
robur : et, ut iussos cunctari vidit, ab uno
edidit haec rapta sceleratus verba securi :
" non dilecta deae solum, sed et ipsa licebit   755
sit dea, iam tanget frondente cacumine terram."
    ' Dixit, et obliquos dum telum librat in ictus,
contremuit gemitumque dedit Deoïa quercus :
et pariter frondes, pariter pallescere glandes
coepere ac longi pallorem ducere rami.   760
cuius ut in trunco fecit manus impia vulnus,
haud aliter fluxit discusso cortice sanguis,
quam solet, ante aras ingens ubi victima taurus
concidit, abrupta cruor e cervice profundi.
    ' Obstipuere omnes : aliquisque ex omnibus audet
deterrere nefas, saevamque inhibere bipennem.   766

aspicit hunc " mentis " que " piae cape praemia! "
    dixit
Thessalus inque virum convertit ab arbore ferrum,
detruncatque caput ; repetitaque robora caedit,
redditus et medio sonus est de robore talis :   770
" nympha sub hoc ego sum Cereri gratissima ligno,
quae tibi factorum poenas instare tuorum
vaticinor moriens, nostri solacia leti."
   ' Persequitur scelus ille suum, labefactaque tan-
    dem
ictibus innumeris adductaque funibus arbor   775
corruit et multam prostravit pondere silvam.

How Erysichthon, for his sin, was smitten by Ceres
with insatiable hunger

attonitae Dryades damno nemorumque suoque
omnes germanae, Cererem cum vestibus atris
maerentes adeunt poenamque Erysichthonis orant.
adnuit his, capitisque sui pulcherrima motu   780
concussit gravidis oneratos messibus agros ;
moliturque genus poenae miserabile, si non
ille suis esset nulli miserabilis actis,
pestifera lacerare Fame. quae quatenus ipsi
non adeunda deae est (neque enim Cereremque
    Famemque   785
fata coire sinunt) montani numinis unam
talibus agrestem compellat Oreada dictis :
" est locus extremis Scythiae glacialis in oris,

triste solum, sterilis, sine fruge, sine arbore tellus.
Frigus iners illic habitant Pallorque Tremorque   790
et ieiuna Fames. ea se in praecordia condat
sacrilegi scelerata iube, nec copia rerum
vincat eam, superetque meas certamine vires.
neve viae spatium te terreat, accipe currus,
accipe, quos frenis alte moderere, dracones."   795
et dedit : illa dato subvecta per aëra curru
devenit in Scythiam rigidique cacumine montis
(Caucason appellant) serpentum colla levavit,
quaesitamque Famem lapidoso vidit in agro
unguibus et raras vellentem dentibus herbas.   800
hirtus erat crinis, cava lumina, pallor in ore,
labra incana situ, scabrae rubigine fauces,
dura cutis, per quam spectari viscera possent,
ossa sub incurvis exstabant arida lumbis,
ventris erat pro ventre locus, pendere putares   805
pectus et a spinae tantummodo crate teneri.
auxerat articulos macies, genuumque tumebat
orbis, et immodico prodibant tubere tali.
hanc procul ut vidit (neque enim est accedere iuxta
ausa), refert mandata deae : paulumque morata, 810
quamquam aberat longe, quamquam modo venerat
    illuc,
visa tamen sensisse famem ; retroque dracones
egit in Haemoniam, versis sublimis habenis.
   ' Dicta Fames Cereris, quamvis contraria semper

illius est operi, peragit, perque aëra vento   815
ad iussam delata domum est et protinus intrat
sacrilegi thalamos, altoque sopore solutum
(noctis enim tempus) geminis amplectitur ulnis
seque viro inspirat faucesque et pectus et ora
adflat et in vacuis spargit ieiunia venis.   82◖
functaque mandato fecundum deserit orbem
inque domos inopes, adsueta revertitur antra.

How Erysichthon's hunger drove him at last to sell his daughter
    into slavery ; how she was changed by Neptune, her lover,
    into a man, and how she thereafter had power to assume
    many forms

' Lenis adhuc somnus placidis Erysichthona pennis
mulcebat : petit ille dapes sub imagine somni,
oraque vana movet dentemque in dente fatigat   825
exercetque cibo delusum guttur inani,
proque epulis tenues nequiquam devorat auras.
ut vero est expulsa quies, furit ardor edendi,
perque avidas fauces immensaque viscera regnat.
nec mora : quod pontus, quod terra, quod educat aër,
poscit, et appositis queritur ieiunia mensis,   831
inque epulis epulas quaerit ; quodque urbibus esse,
quodque satis poterat populo, non sufficit uni,
plusque cupit, quo plura suam demittit in alvum.
utque fretum recipit de tota flumina terra,   835
nec satiatur aquis, peregrinosque ebibit amnes,
utque rapax ignis non umquam alimenta recusat,

innumerasque trabes cremat et, quo copia maior
est data, plura petit, turbaque voracior ipsa est :
sic epulas omnes Erysichthonis ora profani   **840**
accipiunt poscuntque simul. cibus omnis in illo
causa cibi est, semperque locus fit inanis edendo.

  ' Iamque fame patrias altaque voragine ventris
attenuarat opes, sed inattenuata manebat
tum quoque dira fames, implacataeque vigebat   **845**
flamma gulae. tandem, demisso in viscera censu,
filia restabat, non illo digna parente.
hanc quoque vendit inops. dominum generosa
    recusat,
et vicina suas tendens super aequora palmas
" eripe me domino, qui raptae praemia nobis   **850**
virginitatis habes " ait : haec Neptunus habebat,
qui prece non spreta, quamvis modo visa sequenti
esset ero, formamque novat vultumque virilem
induit, et cultus pisces capientibus aptos.
hanc dominus spectans " o qui pendentia parvo   **855**
aera cibo celas, moderator harundinis," inquit,
" sic mare compositum, sic sit tibi piscis in unda
credulus, et nullos, nisi fixus, sentiat hamos :
quae modo cum vili turbatis veste capillis
litore in hoc steterat (nam stantem in litore vidi),
dic ubi sit : neque enim vestigia longius exstant."
illa dei munus bene cedere sensit, et a se   **862**
se quaeri gaudens, his est resecuta rogantem :

" quisquis es, ignoscas : in nullam lumina partem
gurgite ab hoc flexi studioque operatus inhaesi.   865
quoque minus dubites, sic has deus aequoris artes
adiuvet, ut nemo iamdudum litore in isto,
me tamen excepto, nec femina constitit ulla."
credidit, et verso dominus pede pressit harenam
elususque abiit.   illi sua reddita forma est.   870
   ' Ast ubi habere suam transformia corpora sensit,
saepe pater dominis Triopeïda tradit.   at illa
nunc equa, nunc ales, modo bos, modo cervus abibat
praebebatque avido non iusta alimenta parenti.
vis tamen illa mali postquam consumpserat omnem
materiam, dederatque gravi nova pabula morbo,   876
ipse suos artus lacero divellere morsu
coepit, et infelix minuendo corpus alebat.
   ' Quid moror externis? etiam mihi saepe novandi
     est
corporis, o iuvenis, numero finita potestas.   880
nam modo qui nunc sum videor, modo flector in
     anguem,
armenti modo dux vires in cornua sumo ;
cornua, dum potui.   nunc pars caret altera telo
frontis, ut ipse vides.'   gemitus sunt verba secuti.

NOTES

Lines 1, 2. retegente ... fugante ... Lucifero, ablative absolute. Translate by a time clause : ' While Lucifer revealed ... and put to flight ...'

l. 2. tempora, ' hours '.

l. 4. Aeacidis, dat. pl. : the Aeacidae, or ' sons of Aeacus ', were Peleus and Telamon. They are in command of a contingent of men sent by their father, the King of Aegina, to help the Athenians, who are at war with Minos, King of Crete.

l. 4. Cephalo : an Athenian, sent as ambassador to the court of Aegina to request help against Minos.

l. 4. quibus feliciter acti, lit. ' favourably propelled by which '. quibus is an ablative of the instrument and refers to **Austri.** acti agrees with the subject of **tenuere.**

l. 5. ante exspectatum, ' sooner than expectation ', i.e. ' before they were expected '. **exspectatum** is acc. sg. neut. of the perf. partic. pass. of **exspecto,** and is here used as a noun.

l. 5. portus petitos, ' the harbour sought ', i.e. ' the harbour which they were seeking '. Note (i) the plural **portus.** One of the most frequent licences adopted by the Latin poets is the use of the plural for the singular, the reason being generally one of metrical convenience. Can you see why the plural is preferred to the singular in this place? (ii) the use of the participle **petitos** as equivalent to a relative clause.

l. 5. tenuere = tenuerunt. This form of the 3rd pl. perf. indic. act. is very common in poetry.

l. 6. Lelegeïa (five syllables) =' Megarian '. The Leleges were an aboriginal people of Greece, believed to have left traces of their occupation in the country about Megara. It is characteristic of Latin poetry to refer thus obliquely to persons and places in a way that a highly educated audience alone would understand and appreciate. Comparable in our own language is the use of the adjective ' Milesian ' for Irish.

l. 7. sui Mavortis, ' of his host ' (depending on **vires,** ' strength '). The name of the god—**Mavors** = Mars—is used here for the thing with which he is in worship associated, i.e. ' war ', ' army '. This is another very common feature of Latin poetry, and in its allusiveness is similar to the use of literary epithets such as **Lelegeïus** above. Other examples frequently met are **Venus** for ' love ', **Bacchus** for ' wine ', and **Volcanus** for ' fire '. In the present book, l. 292, we have Ceres standing for ' bread '. This figure of speech is called *metonymy*.

ll. 7, 8. urbe Alcathoi. ' The city of Alcathous ' is Megara, whose walls were rebuilt by Alcathous with the help of Apollo. This is yet another instance of the allusive quality of Latin poetry, remarked upon in the notes on **Lelegeïa** and **Mavortis** above.

Presumably Megara is attacked by Minos as an ally of Athens.

l. 8. Nisus was King of Megara, and a brother of Aegeus the Athenian king.

l. 8. cui . . . inhaerebat (l. 10). The order for translation is, ' **cui inter honoratos canos, medioque in vertice, inhaerebat crinis splendidus ostro.**

l. 8. cui =' whose '. The use of the dative where we should expect a possessive genitive is extremely common in Latin.

l. 8. crinis splendidus ostro, ' a lock bright with purple ' We should say ' of bright purple '.

l. 10. fiducia is in apposition to **crinis.**

E

l. 11. **Sexta** is used as an adv., ' for the sixth time '. The meaning is, ' It was the sixth day of the new moon '.

l. 13. **utrumque,** probably masculine and referring to Minos and Nisus.

l. 13. **dubiis pennis.** Victory was usually represented in ancient art as a winged figure.

l. 14. **addita,** ' built upon '.   •

l. 14. **vocalibus.** Why the walls are called ' musical ' is made clear in ll. 15, 16.

l. 15. **proles Letoïa.** ' The child of Leto ' (=Latona) is Apollo. A more simple example of literary allusiveness.

l. 15. **fertur,** ' is said '. Note this meaning of **fero.**

l. 16. **saxo,** i.e. in the stone on which the lyre was laid. **saxo** is dative. Compound verbs are very frequently constructed with this case.

l. 16. **eius** =lyrae.

l. 17. **illuc,** i.e. to the tower mentioned in l. 14.

l. 17. **filia Nisi.** She was called Scylla.

l. 18. **petere,** ' aim at '; **saxa,** pl. for sg., cf. note on l. 5.

l. 19. **tum cum pax esset,** ' in the days when there was peace '.

l. 19. **bello,** abl. of time when, ' in war '.

l. 20. **illa** =turri.

l. 20. **Martis,** ' war '.   Cf. note on **Mavortis,** l. 7.

l. 21. **mora,** abl. of cause, ' owing to the length '.

l. 21. **norat,** a syncopated, i.e. shortened, form of **noverat,** pluperfect of **nosco** =' she knew '.

l. 22. **Cydoneas.** Cydonia was a town in Crete. Cretan archers were so famous that words for bows and arrows were very often qualified by literary epithets, which, like **Cydoneus,** suggest Crete, even when there was not, as here there is a real connection.

l. 23. **Europaei.** ' The son of Europa ' is Minos.

l. 24. **nosse** = novisse, ' to know '. Another syncopated form. The principle of these forms is that a ' v ', and sometimes the following vowel, are dropped out. Cf. **norat**, l. 21.

l. 24. **sat**, ' good '.

l. 24. **hac iudice**, ablative absolute, ' with her (as) judge ', i.e. ' in her judgment '.

l. 25. **casside**, ablative of the instrument, but we should say ' in (or under) his helmet '.

l. 25. **cristata pennis**, ' crested wtih plumes ', i.e. ' plume-crested '.

l. 27. **sumpsisse decebat**, ' it became (him) to have taken ', i.e. ' the taking up of his shield became him '.

l. 28. **torserat**. In English we should begin this sentence (and similarly l. 30) with ' if ', and make the clauses subordinate to those which follow in ll. 29, 31.

l. 28. **adducere lacertos** is ' to bend the arm '. Notice the plural **lacertos** for the singular.

l. 29. **iunctam cum viribus artem**, lit., ' skill joined with strength, ' or, as we should say, ' the union of strength and skill '.

l. 30. **imposito**, placed, that is, upon the bow-string. **imposito calamo** is ablative absolute. **arcus**, pl. for sg. again.

l. 31. **Phoebum stare**, accusative and infinitive depending on **iurabat**.

l. 31. **sumptis sagittis**, abl. abs., ' when he has taken ', etc.

l. 32. **nudaverat**. **cum** when followed by the pluperfect *indicative* means ' whenever '.

l. 32. **aere**, ' his bronze ' = ' his helmet of bronze '.

ll. 33, 34. **purpureusque . . . equi**, ' and clothed-in-purple sat (premebat) the back of his white steed, caparisoned (insignia) with embroidered saddle-cloth '.

l. 35. **sua**, ' her own ', i.e. ' mistress of herself '.

l. 35. **sanae compos mentis**, ' in control of her wits '.

l. 36. **felix** and **felicia,** l. 37, are predicative. ' She called the javelin happy,' etc.

l. 36. **quod** is ' which ', not ' because ', as **quaeque** (=**quae,** rel., +-**que**) in l. 37 shows.

l. 36. **tangeret** and **premeret,** l. 37, are best regarded as subjunctives of virtual Oratio Obliqua, that is, they are in the subjunctive because they are part of Scylla's, not the author's, thought. Cf. **Puerum magister culpavit quod pensum non confecisset :** ' The master blamed the boy, because (*as the master said*) he had not completed his task '.

l. 38. **impetus est illi,** ' there is to her a prompting ', **i.e.** ' she feels an impulse '. **illi** is dative of the possessor.

l. 38. **liceat modo,** ' if she but may ', lit. ' let it only be permitted '. **liceat** may be regarded as an *optative* use of the subjunctive, i.e. a subjunctive expressing a wish.

ll. 38, 39. **ferre virgineos gradus,** ' to carry her maiden steps ', i.e. ' to make her maiden way '.

l. 40. **turribus,** pl. for sg.

l. 40. **Gnosia,** i.e. ' Cretan ', since Gnosus or Gnossus was the capital city of Minos, king of Crete. This is another allusive, literary, epithet.

l. 42. **vel . . . siquid.** Assume that **facere** is to be inserted between these words.

l. 42. **siquid** =**quidquid,** ' whatever '.

l. 42. **aliud,** ' else '.

l. 42. **ut** +indicative =' as ' (as here) or ' when '.

l. 43. **Dictaei.** The adjective derives from Mount Dicte in Crete, and therefore ' the Dictaean king ' (i.e. Minos) is one more illustration of the allusiveness so often noted.

ll. 44, 45. **laeter doleamne in dubio est,** ' it is in doubt whether I should rejoice or grieve '. **laeter doleamne** are alternative indirect deliberative questions depending on **in dubio est.** In prose we should expect **laeterne an doleam.**

l. 44. **geri bellum,** acc. +inf., ' that war,' etc.

l. 45. **dubio,** the neuter of the adjective is here used as a noun.

l. 45. **amanti,** ' to his lover '. Scylla is referring, of course, to herself. Note the use of the present participle **amans** as a noun.

l. 46. **bella,** pl. for sg.   **forent = essent.**

The subjunctives **forent, cognitus esset** are conditional : ' but if war were not, he would never have been known to me '. Notice the use of the imperfect and pluperfect subjunctives for assumptions contrary to fact, in present and past time respectively (the facts being that there *is* war and he *has been made known*).

ll. 47, 48. **me accepta obside,** abl. abs., equivalent to the protasis of a conditional sentence, ' if he received me (as) a hostage '. Notice that in such cases as this, where English requires ' as ', Latin is content with placing the two nouns (or, as here, pronoun and noun) in apposition. Cf. **comitem** and **pignus,** in apposition with **me,** l. 48.

l. 47. **deponere :** so we too might speak of ' dropping ' a war.

l. 47. **poterat.** Note the use of the *imperfect* indicative. It implies that the possibility, which still exists, has also for some time existed.

l. 48. **haberet.** Cf. note on **forent,** l. 46.

l. 49. **si quae,** ' if (she) who . . .' The mother of Minos was Europa, and his father, Jupiter.

l. 49. **pulcherrimĕ,** voc. sg. masc.

l. 49. **talis** is complement of **fuit** and antecedent to **qualis,** ' was such as '.

l. 49. **rerum,** ' of creatures '.

l. 50. **deus,** Jupiter.

l. 50. **arsit in illa. ardere in aliquā** is ' to be smitten with love for someone '.

l. 51. **ō ĕgŏ,** dactyl.   The **ō** is not elided.

l. 51. **ter felix.** Supply **essem,** ' I should be '.

l. 52. **Gnosiaci**, ' Cretan '. Cf. note on l. 40.

l. 53. Take the words in the order : **rogarem qua dote vellet emi**, ' and inquire for what dowry he was willing to be bought ', i.e. as her husband.

l. 54. **tantum ... arces.** This depends on **rogarem in a** slightly different meaning, ' beg '. ' And beg him only not demand '.

l. 55. **pereant, sim,** optative subjunctives expressing wishes, ' may ... be lost ', etc.

l. 55. **cubilia** (subj. of **pereant**). There are two poetic figures here, (i) pl. for sg. ; (ii) the word is used by association for ' marriage '.

l. 56. **potens.** The usual expression is **potens voti**, ' master of one's desire ', i.e. ' satisfied '. Scylla means she would rather give up her desire to marry Minos than attain it by treachery.

ll. 56, 57. **quamvis ... multis.** She nevertheless begins at once to seek justification for the act of betrayal she has just repudiated. ' Yet the mercy of an appeased conqueror has often made defeat (**vinci**) profitable to many.'

l. 56. **vinci**, ' to be conquered ' (=' defeat ') is direct object of **fecit**, and **utile** predicate to it.

l. 56. **quamvis**, ' yet ', not ' although '. This would account for the indicative ' **fecit** ', since **quamvis** usually takes the subjunctive.

l. 58. **pro nato perempto**, ' for his murdered son '. The son referred to is Androgeus. Having aroused the envy of the Athenians by his prowess at their games, he was assassinated. It was in revenge for his murder that Minos was engaged in the war with Athens, in which struggle the siege of Megara, the theme of the present story, was an incident.

l. 58. **iusta bella**, pl. for sg.

l. 59. **et ... -que ... -que**, ' and ... both ... and '.

l. 59. **causa** and **armis** are abls. of respect, ' in his cause ', ' in the arms '.

l. 59. **valet.** Minos is the subject, as also of **gerit**, l. 58.

l. 59. **tuentibus**, ' which defend '. Cf. note (ii) on **portus petitos**, l. 5.

l. 60. **qui.** The use of the relative to begin a fresh sentence is unnatural in English. Translate by ' this '.

It is interesting to see how readily Scylla seeks specious arguments in favour of a course she knows to be wrong.

l. 61. **Mavors**, ' force ' or ' army '. Cf. note on l. 7.

l. 61. **illi**, dative of advantage.

l. 61. **reseret**, deliberative subjunctive, ' should unbar '.

l. 62. **noster**, ' my ', in spite of having used **mea** with **moenia** in the previous line.

l. 63. **impensā**, like **caede** and **mora**, is governed by **sine**.

l. 63. **poterit.** Minos is still the subject.

l. 64. **metuam**, fut. ' I shall not have to fear ' (i.e. if she brings about the betrayal she intends).

l. 64. **pectora**, pl. for sg.

l. 65. **imprudens**, ' unaware '. She cannot, in her infatuation, believe that anyone could wound her hero ' of set purpose ' (**non inscius**, 66).

l. 65. **tam durus**, supply **est.**

ll. 67, 68. **secum dotalem patriam**, ' her country, together with herself, as-dowry '.

l. 69. **velle** is subject of **est**, **parum** the complement.

l. 69. **aditus**, acc. pl.

l. 72. **di . . . forem.** ' O that the gods acted so that I were without a father ! ' i.e. ' Would to God I had no father ! ' **facerent** is optative subjunctive and **forem** may be taken as dependent upon it, with **ut** suppressed.

l. 72. **profecto**, adv. ' surely '. The sense is that prayer is useless and that mortals must each bring their own desires to fruition.

l. 74. **altera**, ' another woman '.

ll. 74, 75. **iamdudum gauderet**, ' would long since have

delighted '. The protasis (*if*-clause) to this conditional is contained in the participle **succensa,** ' if she had been fired '.

l. 75. obstaret. Either generic subjunctive, i.e. a subjunctive used in a relative clause where no precise antecedent is thought of, or possibly subjunctive by attraction, i.e. in sympathy with the preceding subjunctive **gauderet.**

l. 76. foret, ' should be '.

l. 76. me, abl. of comparison, ' than I '.

l. 76. per ignes et gladios, ' through fire and battle '.

l. 77. ausim, potential (i.e. conditional without protasis expressed), ' I would dare '. ausim is an old Latin form, a survival of a future subjunctive. Such forms are rare outside poetry.

l. 77. in hoc, ' in this case '.

l. 78. opus est + abl., ' there is need of '; opus est mihi + abl. = ' I need '.

l. 78. crine. See ll. 8-10. If the **magni fiducia regni** were removed, the fortunes of Nisus would decay.

l. 79. auro, abl. of comparison, ' than gold '.

l. 80. factura, sc. est, ' shall make '.

l. 80. voti mei potentem, ' mistress of my desire '. Cf. note, l. 56.

l. 81. dicenti, dative dependent on **intervenit,** ' upon-her-as-she-uttered . . . came,' etc.

l. 81. curarum maxima nutrix, ' chief nourisher of desire '. nutrix is in apposition to nox.

l. 83. qua, ' in which ', abl. of time when.

l. 84. thalamos, pl. for sg.

l. 84. taciturna, adj. for adv., ' silently '.

l. 85. heu facinus, ' Oh, evil deed! '

l. 85. nata, ' she, his daughter '.

l. 86. crine, abl. of separation with **spoliat,** ' robs of his lock '.

l. 86. praeda nefanda, abl., governed by **potita.**

l. 88. meriti fiducia, ' confidence in her deserving ', **i.e.** she feels that her service to Minos in presenting him with the lock ensures her a good reception.

When the relation between one noun and another in the genitive case is, as here, similar to that between a verb and its object (in this case **fido** and **meritum**) the use of the genitive is called objective. Cf. **amor patris,** ' love for one's father '.

l. 89. quem. Cf. note on **qui,** l. 60, and translate by ' him '.

l. 89. paventem, ' horrified '.

l. 91. patriae ... penates, ' my country's guardian spirit and my own '. The lock is rather the *token* of divine protection.

l. 92. pignus, ' (as) a pledge '. Cf. note on **obside,** l. 48.

l. 93. The order for translation is **nec crede me nunc tibi tradere.** Note the use of the imperative **crede** in a negative command, a construction inadmissible in prose.

l. 94. caput, ' life '.

l. 94. dextra, abl. of the instrument, ' with her right hand '.

l. 95. munera, pl. for sg.

l. 95. porrecta, sc. **munera,** ' the proffered (gift) '. Translate by ' offering '.

l. 96. The sinister meaning given here, and often in Latin, to **novus,**—' strange ', almost ' dreadful '—is an indication of Roman conservatism, showing that innovation tended to be regarded with suspicion.

l. 97. summoveant, negetur. Optative subjunctives again, ' may the gods,' etc.

l. 98. orbe suo, ' from their own world ', i.e. the sky and the air.

l. 98. negetur. Note the singular verb, in spite of its two subjects, **tellus** and **pontus.**

l. 99. patiar, future.

l. 99. Iovis incunabula. Jupiter, according to mythology, was, as a new-born babe, hidden in Crete from his father

Saturn, who sought to devour all his children, it having been prophesied that one of them should bring about his fall.

l. 99. **Creten.** **-n** is the termination of the accusative singular in the Greek 1st declension.

l. 100. **qui.** As usual in Latin, the relative pronoun agrees, not with its antecedent (**Creten**, *fem.*), but with the complement of the verb **sum** (**orbis**, *masc.*).

l. 100. **contingere,** ' to suffer contact with ', as it would if he took Scylla to wife.

l. 101. **ut,** ' when '.

l. 101. **leges,** ' terms '. We are to understand that the cutting of the lock brought about the fall of Megara.

l. 101. **auctor,** ' law-giver ', i.e. Minos, who had so great a reputation for justice that he was believed to have become after his death one of the three judges in Hades.

ll. 101, 102. **captis hostibus,** dative of disadvantage, after **imposuit.**

l. 102. **imposuit.** We should say ' had imposed '.

l. 103. **aeratas,** ' of bronze ', an epithet referring to the bronze armour of the ancient ship's ram.

l. 103. **remige,** sg. for pl., ' rowers '.

l. 104. **freto,** abl. of place, which is often found in poetry without a preposition : ' upon the sea '.

l. 104. **postquam,** ' when '—usually the best translation.

l. 104. **deductas nare carinas,** acc. and inf. dependent on **vidit** : ' that the ships (lit. keels) (were) launched (and) were afloat '.

l. 105. **praestare ducem** is similarly dependent on **vidit.**

l. 105. **ducem** =Minos.

l. 105. **sceleris** depends on **praemia.**

l. 106. **consumptis precibus,** abl. abs.

l. 107. **manus,** acc. pl.

l. 107. **passis,** from **pando.**

l. 107. **capillis,** abl.

l. 108. **quo,** adv., ' whither '. Similarly in l. 113.

l. 108. **meritorum auctore relicta,** abl. abs., ' abandoning the author of thy success '. She means, of course, herself.

l. 109. **praelate,** from **praefero**—parse carefully. ' O thou, whom I preferred '.

l. 110. **immitis,** voc. sg., ' cruel one '.

l. 111. **data.** The participle here, as often, is equivalent to a relative clause, ' which I gave '.

l. 112. **noster,** ' my '.

l. 112. **quod,** ' *the fact* that '.

l. 112. **unum = solum.**

l. 113. **congesta est,** ' was centred '.

l. 114. **finge manere.** Supply **eam** (= **patriam**) as acc. subject to the infin. **manere.** ' Imagine that it still existed '.

l. 115. **ora,** pl. for sg.

l. 116. **odere = oderunt.** Remember that the perfect tense of this defective verb is present in meaning.

l. 116. **merentem,** lit. ' deserving '. Translate as an adv., ' deservedly '.

l. 117. **exemplum,** ' the example (I have set) '. The neighbours fear to give Scylla sanctuary lest other women, reminded by her presence of what has occurred, should commit similar treachery.

l. 117. **orbe,** abl. of place whence, ' from the world '. Note that **orbis terrarum** is the regular Latin for ' world '.

l. 118. **pateret,** final. Note the unusual sequence.

l. 118. **nobis,** pl. for sg.

l. 119. **hanc = Creten. nos,** pl. for sg.

l. 120. **genetrix tibi,** ' your mother ', the possessive being often thus expressed by a dative.

l. 120. **Syrtis,** the name of a dangerous sand-bank off the

N. coast of Africa. Scylla professes to believe him the off-spring of some inhuman thing, or of an animal.

l. 121. **tigres,** pl. for sg.

l. 121. **Charybdis,** a celebrated whirlpool in the straits between Italy and Sicily.

l. 122. **Iove,** abl. of origin. **natus,** supply **es.** ' Nor art thou a son of Jove '.

l. 122. **imagine tauri.** Jove was said to have appeared to Europa, the mother of Minos, in the form of a white bull, and to have lured her on his back over the sea to Crete.

l. 123. **ducta,** ' beguiled '.

l. 123. **generis,** sc. **tui.**

ll. 123-125. The order is **taurus, qui te progenuit, fuit verus** (' real ') **et ferus et captus amore nullius iuvencae.**

l. 126. **malis,** abl. pl. neut., ' miseries '. The abl. is abl. of cause, depending on **gaudete,** ' rejoice *at* '.

l. 127. **moenia,** voc. **modo prodita,** ' lately betrayed ', goes with **moenia.**

l. 127. **digna perire.** The infinitive after **dignus** is poetic. In prose we should have **quae** + subjunctive.

l. 128. **impia,** ' unnatural (creature) '. **pietas** is the natural affection of parent for child, child for parent, spouse for spouse, citizen for community, etc. Our word ' piety ' derives from a further meaning, the natural dutifulness of a creature towards his God.

l. 129. **perimat,** jussive subjunctive, ' let . . .'

l. 129. **qui.** The antecedent is **tu** (i.e. Minos), subject of **insequeris.**

l. 129. **crimine nostro,** abl. of means, ' through my sin '.

l. 130. **scelus hoc,** etc., ' let this (i.e. her treachery) be, in the eyes of my country and my father, a crime : in yours, a service '. **patriae, patri, tibi,** are datives of the person judging. Cf. **mihi formosa est,** ' for me (=in my judgment) she is beautiful '.

l. 131. **sit,** jussive subjunctive.

l. 131. **ecquid,** acc. of extent, ' at all ', lit. ' any ', which is an Americanism in the same sense.

l. 135. **ferunt,** ' bear *away* '.

l. 135. **idemque,** ' as well as '. Grammatically **idem** agrees with a second **venti** understood, ' and do the same (winds) bear . . .'

l. 138. **me miseram,** acc. of exclamation. Translate by ' woe is me! '

l. 138. **iuvat,** ' it pleases (him) ', i.e. ' 'tis his pleasure '.

l. 139. **sonat,** ' ripples '.

l. 139. **recedit,** i.e. from Minos, as his ships leave the land.

l. 140. **nil agis,** ' thou gainest (*lit.* dost) naught '.

l. 140. **oblite,** parse carefully.

l. 141. **invitum** agrees with **te** (object of **insequar**) understood.

l. 142. **vix dixerat, insilit,** ' scarce had she ceased to speak (when) she . . . '

l. 142. **undis,** poetic dative of motion towards, ' into the waves '.

l. 143. **faciente cupidine vires,** abl. abs., ' her passion lending her (*lit.* making) strength '.

l. 144. **Gnosiacae carinae,** dative, depending on **haeret.**

l. 144. **comes invidiosa,** nom. in apposition to ' she ', subject of **haeret.**

l. 145. **quam,** ' her '. Cf. note on l. 89.

l. 145. **ut,** ' when '.

l. 145. **pendebat,** ' was hovering '.

l. 146. **haliaeetos,** predicative to **factus erat,** ' had been made an osprey '.

l. 147. **ibat,** ' began to swoop '. The imperfect tense in Latin sometimes denotes the commencement of action.

l. 147. **haerentem,** ' (her) clinging ', i.e. ' her as she clung '.

l. 147. **laceraret,** final subjunctive.

l. 148. **metu,** abl. of cause, ' in fear '.

l. 148. **cadentem.** Translate similarly to **haerentem,** l. 147.

l. 149. **sustinuisse.** The perfect infinitive is sometimes used in poetry in a meaning indistinguishable from the present.

l. 150. **pluma fuit,** ' it was her plumage ' that sustained her, for she too had been ' changed into a bird '.

l. 151. **a tonso capillo.** ' from the shorn lock ', or as we should say ' from the shearing of the lock '. Ovid derives the name **ciris** from the Greek word κείρω, I cut, shear.

l. 152. **Minos,** king of Crete, whose conquest of Megara through the treachery of Scylla, daughter of the Megarian king, is the subject of ll. 1-151 of this book, had vowed a hundred oxen to Jove in the event of his success in war against Athens.

l. 152. **corpora** is in apposition to **vota** (acc.). The sacrifice of a hundred oxen was called a hecatomb.

l. 153. **solvit,** perfect.

l. 153. **ut,** ' when '. In this meaning, and also that of ' as ', **ut** regularly takes the indicative.

l. 153. **ratibus,** abl. of place whence, going with **egressus.** Constructions such as this, which would require prepositions in prose, are frequently used without them in poetry. The word **ratis,** which properly means ' a raft ', is common in poetry in the meaning ' ship '. Cf. English ' bark '.

l. 153. **Curetida.** The ending is that of the accusative case in the Greek 3rd declension. **Curetida** agrees with **terram,** and stands for ' Cretan ', because the Curetes, according to mythology, dwelt in that island. But it is very usual for Ovid and indeed most poets, not merely Latin ones, to refer to things in this oblique, allusive way. Compare the use in our own tongue of ' Milesian ' for Irish, from Milesius, a legendary king supposed to have colonized Ireland from Spain.

l. 154. **spoliis fixis,** ' with trophies set up ', **i.e.** ' by setting up trophies '. The decoration of English homes with such souvenirs of war is not unknown.

l. 154. **fixis.** Notice how the Latin participle agreeing with a noun is here equivalent to an English gerund and its noun object. Cf. a similar use of the participle in **Caesar interfectus plebem perturbavit,** ' the murder of Caesar (*lit.* C. having been murdered) troubled the common people '.

l. 155. **creverat,** i.e. while Minos was absent at the wars.

l. 155. **opprobrium generis,** this ' reproach of (we should say ' to ') his family ' was the Minotaur, a creature half man, half bull, illegitimate offspring of Minos' wife, Pasiphae.

l. 155. **foedumque patebat,** lit., ' and was obvious loathsome ', i.e. ' in his loathsomeness '.

l. 157. **thalamis,** ' from his chamber '. The plural is here used for the singular. This is one of the most common licences of Latin poetry, arising from the difficulty of composing in a foreign (Greek) metre unsuited to the nature of the Latin tongue. For the ablative of place whence without a preposition, cf. **ratibus,** l. 153.

l. 158. **multiplici,** etc. This ' house of-manifold-passages and dwelling dark ' is the famous Labyrinth.

l. 158. **tectis** is another case of pl. for sg.

l. 158. **includere,** like **removere,** l. 157, governs **hunc pudorem,** i.e. the Minotaur.

l. 159. **Daedalus** is the great craftsman of mythology, and reputed to have been the first aeronaut. An Athenian, he lived and was employed at the court of Minos.

l. 159. **ingenio fabrae artis,** ' for his talent in the craft of carpentry '. The genitive **artis** is not readily classified, but difficult uses of the case are not uncommon, as it is used to express almost any relation between one noun and another.

l. 160. **ponit,** ' builds '.

l. 160. **turbatque notas,** ' confuses the signs ', i.e. ' makes all marks of direction indistinguishable '.

l. 160. lumina, ' eyes ', a very common meaning in poetry.

l. 160. flexum . . . in errorem, ' into wandering this way and that '.

l. 162. non secus ac, ' not otherwise than ', i.e. ' even as '.

l. 162. Phrygius Maeandrus. The Maeander, a river of Phrygia in Asia Minor, was proverbial in the ancient world for its winding course. Hence the English noun and verb, ' meander '.

l. 164. ' and meeting himself looks on the waters yet to come ', i.e. bends back until close to a reach of the river nearer the source.

l. 165. fontes, pl. for sg.

l. 165. versus, participle of vertor used as a deponent, and therefore capable of present meaning : ' turning '.

l. 166. exercet, ' drives '.

l. 167. errore, sg. for pl. this time.

l. 167. vias, ' passages '.

l. 167. vixque, etc. The maze almost entrapped its own creator.

l. 169. quo. It is common in Latin to begin fresh sentences with relatives having their antecedents in a previous sentence. In this case we have to go back to opus in l. 160. Translate ' in it '.

l. 169. postquam. The best translation is, as usual, 'when'.

l. 169. geminam tauri iuvenisque figuram, i.e. the Minotaur.

l. 170. clausit, ' had imprisoned '. The aorist-perfect, not the pluperfect as in English, is regular after postquam. Note also domuit, l. 171, which also depends on postquam.

l. 170. et Actaeo . . . relecto (l. 173). After his conquest of Athens, in revenge for the assassination of his son Androgeos, who had roused Athenian jealousy by his successes at their games, Minos imposed on the defeated city a tribute, at intervals of nine years, of seven maids and seven youths, to be devoured by the ferocious Minotaur. The victims were chosen by lot (sors). When the third occasion for paying the tribute arose, Theseus, son of the Athenian king, voluntarily accompanied the selected victims. By the aid of Ariadne, daughter of Minos, who had become infatuated with him, and supplied him with a sword and a clew of thread with which to retrace his steps out of the Labyrinth, Theseus slew the Minotaur and returned in safety.

ll. 170-171. ' and the third lot, renewed every nine years, had laid low the monster twice fed on Attic blood '. **Actaeo,** ' Attic ', because Acte was an old name for Attica, the country about Athens. For the adjective cf. note on **Curetida,** l. 153.

l. 172. **utque,** ' and when '. The principal clause begins at **protinus,** l. 174.

l. 172. **virginea.** The reference is to Ariadne.

l. 172. **nullis,** ' by none ', dative of the agent dependent on **iterata.** This use of the case is not uncommon in poetry with the perf. partic. pass.

l. 172. **priorum,** ' of his predecessors ', i.e. of those who before him had attempted to find their way out of the Labyrinth.

l. 173. **filo relecto,** ' by the thread which he wound up '.

l. 174. **Aegides,** ' the son of Aegeus ', i.e. Theseus. -ides is a Greek patronymic termination =' son of '.

l. 174. **Minoide,** abl. of Minois, daughter of Minos, i.e. Ariadne.

l. 174. **Diam** is accusative of motion towards, regularly found without a preposition even in prose, in the case of the names of towns and small islands. Dia is another name for Naxos, an island in the Aegean.

l. 175. **-que.** We should say ' but '.

l. 175. **crudelis,** ' cruelly '. It is not unusual for a Latin writer to put an adjective where we should expect an adverb.

F

l. 175. in illo litore, i.e. on Naxos.

l. 176. desertae et ... querenti. These participles agree with ei (=Ariadne) understood.

l. 176. multa querenti, ' complaining many (complaints) ', i.e. ' uttering many a plaint '. multa is adverbial accusative.

l. 177. amplexus. Scan, to determine whether this word is participle, (-ŭs), or noun, (-ūs).

l. 178. clara, ' renowned '.

l. 178. foret (=esset) final subjunctive. The subject is probably Ariadne.

l. 178. sumptam coronam immisit, ' placed the crown having been taken ',—the regular Latin way of saying ' took the crown and placed (it) '.

l. 179. illa, i.e. the crown.

l. 180. dumque, ' and as '.

l. 181. loco, ' in a place '.

l. 182. ' which is mid-way between the Kneeler and him that grasps the Serpent '. The reference is to two other constellations, that of Hercules, which is likened to a man ' supported by his knee ' (nixus genu) and of Ophiuchus, a Greek word of which anguem tenens is a translation. For the genitives Nixi and tenentis, cf. note on artis, l. 159.

l. 183. Creten. The ending -n is that of the acc. sg. in the Greek 1st declension.

l. 183. perosus. The perfect participle of the defective verb odi is used in an active and present sense, ' loathing '.

l. 184. loci natalis, i.e. Athens. loci is a good example of the objective genitive. This name is given where the relation of a genitive to the noun on which it depends is similar to that between a direct object and its verb, in this case between locum and amare.

l. 185. clausus erat pelago, because, of course, Crete is an island.

l. 185. licet. The word is a conjunction here, meaning

' although ', and taking the subjunctive. The meaning
' although ' derives easily enough from the usual ' it is
permitted ', which approximates to ' granted that '.

l. 186. **obstruat.** The subject is Minos.

l. 186. **at,** ' yet '.

l. 186. **illac** = caelo.

l. 187. **possideat,** concessive subjunctive, ' though he pos-
sesses '.

l. 187. **aëra,** acc. sg., formed according to the Greek third
declension, of **aër.**

l. 189. **novat,** ' changes ', i.e. by becoming a bird-man.
The next few lines describe the construction of the wings.

l. 190. **a minima coeptas,** ' begun (we should say ' beginning ') with the smallest '.

l. 190. **longam breviore sequenti,** abl. abs., ' a shorter
(one) coming after a long (one) '. As Ovid describes
Daedalus as having begun with the shortest, we should
expect him to proceed rather from short to longer, and say
brevem longiore sequenti. This, however, would not scan.
sequenti is unusual. The abl. sg. of the present participle
is usually in -e, unless the use is purely adjectival.

l. 191. **ut clivo crevisse putes.** Supply **eas** as subject to
the infinitive **crevisse** : ' so that you would think they had
grown upon a hill-side '. Ovid compares the appearance of
the feathers thus arranged to a wood growing upon a slope,
with the upper trees projecting above the lower.

l. 191. **sic rustica quondam,** etc. Here the graduated
feathers are compared to the several uneven reeds of a
shepherd's pipe. **quondam,** ' sometimes '.

l. 193. **alligat.** The subject is Daedalus.

l. 193. **medias et imas,** sc. **pennas,** ' at the middle and the
bottom '.

l. 193. **ceris,** pl. for sg.

l. 194. **ita compositas flectit,** ' and bends them, thus
arranged '.

l. 194. parvo curvamine, abl. of manner, ' in . . .'

l. 195. unā, adv.

l. 196. se tractare, acc. and infin. dependent on ignarus, ' unaware *that* '.

l. 196. sua pericla, lit. ' his own dangers ', i.e. ' what was to endanger his own life '.

l. 197. renidenti, adjectival ; cf. note on sequenti, l. 190.

l. 197. modo . . . modo, ' now . . . now '.

l. 197. quas . . . aura. Take this relative clause after captabat plumas, l. 198.

l. 199. mollibat, an archaic form = molliebat.

l. 200. postquam. Cf. note on this word, l. 169.

l. 200. manus, ' touch '.

l. 201. in = ' upon '.

l. 202. mota in aura. ' on the moved air ', i.e. ' on the air, beaten by his wings '.

l. 203. instruit, ' equips '.

l. 203. medio limite, abl. of route or direction, ' upon a mid-way course ', i.e. between the too low (demissior) and the too high (celsior) courses, both dangerous.

l. 203. curras, ' to fly '. The subjunctive is of indirect command, dependent on moneo. The order is aitque ' moneo ut . . . curras '.

l. 205. gravet, adurat, final subjunctives.

l. 205. ignis, i.e. of the sun.

l. 206. inter utrumque, i.e. inter undam et ignem.

l. 206. nec iubeo, ' and I bid you not (to) '. Boöten (and Helicen in the next line) : cf. note on Creten, l. 183. The three constellations Boötes (the Waggoner), Helice (the Great Bear) and Orion, were among the guiding stars of ancient mariners, the first two to the North, the third to the South. But Daedalus bids his son ignore them, and follow him instead.

l. 208. **me duce**, abl. abs., ' with me (as) your leader ', i.e. ' with me for guide '.

l. 208. **pariter tradit et accommodat**, lit. ' at the same time he delivers and fits ', i.e. ' while he is delivering,' etc.

l. 208. **volandi**, ' of flying ', gerund. We should say ' *for* flight '. For the genitive cf. note on **artis**, l. 159.

l. 210. **inter opus monitusque**, lit. ' between the work '— of fitting the wings on Icarus—' and the warnings ', i.e. ' as he toiled and warned '.

l. 210. **maduere**, i.e. with tears.

l. 210. **seniles**. The **senex** is Daedalus.

l. 211. **patriae**, nom. pl. fem. of the adjective **patrius**.

l. 211. **manūs**, nom. pl.

l. 212. **non repetenda**, ' destined not to be . . .' **repetenda** is gerundive and qualifies **oscula**.

l. 212. **levatus**, ' raised ', i.e. ' raising himself '.

l. 213. **ante**, adv.

l. 213. **comiti**, i.e. Icarus.

l. 213. **ales**, ' a mother bird ', the relative **quae** indicating the sex of **ales**.

l. 214. **aëra**. Cf. note on this word, l. 187.

l. 215. **hortaturque**, sc. **eum** (=Icarum) **sequi** (the latter for the **ut sequetur** of prose).

l. 215. **damnosas**, ' baneful ', because it results in the destruction of Icarus.

l. 215. **artes**, pl. for sg.

l. 216. **suas**, sc. **alas**.

l. 217. **hos**, object of **vidit**, l. 219.

l. 217. **captat**, present, though three perfects follow. **dum**, ' while ', mostly takes this tense whatever the tense of the principal clause.

l. 218. **innixus**, ' leaning on ', goes both with **pastor** and arator, and governs baculo and stivā, appropriate respectively to them.

l. 219. vidit, obstipuit, credidit, sg. verbs, though there are three subjects aliquis, pastor, arator.

l. 219. quique ... deos. The order is credidit (eos) esse deos qui aethera carpere possent.

l. 219. aethera, acc. sg. of aether. Cf. note on aëra, l. 187.

l. 219. possent. A subjunctive occurs in a relative clause (i) in Oratio Obliqua, (ii) where the meaning is adverbial rather than adjectival. This is a case of (ii), the meaning being causal, 'since they could', and qui is equivalent to cum ei.

l. 220. Iunonia qualifies Samos.

l. 220. laeva parte, 'on the left hand'; dextra (nom.), l. 222, 'on the right'. Trace the course of Daedalus from Crete upon the map facing the title page.

l. 222. erat has three subjects, Samos, Lebinthus, Calymne.

l. 222. melle, abl. of respect, 'in ...'

l. 223. coepit. When a cum clause, though dependent grammatically, is in sense principal, e.g. in such a sentence as 'It was growing dark *when our friends arrived*', the verb is regularly put in the indicative. Such a clause is called an inverse cum clause.

l. 224. ducem, i.e. Daedalus.

l. 224. tractus, 'attracted'.

l. 224. caeli, objective genitive, cf. note on loci, l. 184.

l. 225. altius, comparative adj., 'too high'. Note this, a not uncommon meaning of the comparative degree.

l. 225. egit, 'pursued'.

l. 225. rapidi. rapidus is connected with rapio, and does not always mean 'swift'. Sometimes, as here, the meaning is 'fiery'.

l. 226. pennarum vincula, lit. 'the fastenings of his

wings ', i.e. ' which secured his wings '. **vincula** is in apposition to **ceras.**

l. 227. **tabuerant.** Note the pluperfect between the presents **mollit** and **quatit.** It suggests the suddenness and completeness of the action. Translate by an English simple past.

l. 227. **nudos,** because the wings had fallen off.

l. 228. **remigio,** abl. governed by **carens. remigium,** a collective noun meaning ' oars ', is here used for ' wings '.

l. 228. **percipit,** ' grips '.

l. 229. **ora,** ' lips ', a common poetic meaning of the word in the plural.

l. 229. **patrium,** parse carefully.

l. 230. **quae nomen traxit ab illo,** becoming, that is, the Icarian Sea.

l. 231. **nec iam,** ' no longer '.

l. 232. **qua regione,** local abl. without preposition, ' in . . .'

l. 232. **requiram,** ' am I to seek '. A question expresses doubt as to a course of action is put in the subjunctive, called the deliberative or dubitative subjunctive.

ll. 234, 235. **corpus sepulchro condidit.** We are to assume that the body of Icarus was washed ashore.

l. 234. **sepulchro,** see note on **qua regione,** l. 232.

l. 235. **tellus,** i.e. the island on which Icarus was buried was called Icaria.

l. 235. **sepulti,** sc. **pueri.**

l. 236. **hunc** = Daedalum.

l. 236. **tumulo,** see note on **qua regione,** l. 232.

l. 236. **corpora,** pl. for sg. ; similarly **gaudia,** l. 238.

l. 239. Supply **erat,** with subject **ea** (=perdix), and **erat** again as auxiliary to **visa** and **facta,** l. 240.

l. 240. **avis,** predicative to **facta (erat).**

l. 240. **longum crimen,** ' an everlasting reproach '.

l. 241. huic = Daedalo.

l. 241. fatorum, an easy example of the objective genitive.

l. 241. docendam, gerundive, ' to be instructed '.

l. 242. germana, the sister, that is, of Daedalus.

l. 242. natalibus actis . . . ad praecepta capacis, lit. ' a boy twice six birthdays having been spent, of a mind capacious towards instruction ', i.e. ' a boy of twelve years, with a mind receptive to teaching '. Two common constructions, the ablative and genitive of quality, or description, are here represented. A Latin noun may be described not only by adjectives, but by phrases, consisting of noun and adjective, put either in the ablative or the genitive. Examples are : senex promissa barba, ' an old man with a long beard ' ; vir summae audaciae, ' a man of the greatest daring '.

l. 243. senis is the distributive numeral, properly meaning ' six *each* ', but regularly used where we should expect the cardinal numeral in expressions including a numeral adverb, e.g. bis bina sunt quattuor, ' twice two are four '.

ll. 244-246. He invented the saw.

l. 244. etiam, ' even '.

l. 244. medio spinas in pisce notatas, i.e. the fish's backbone.

l. 245. traxit in exemplum, ' took as a pattern '.

l. 245. ferro, dative after the compound verb incidit.

l. 246. perpetuos dentes, ' endless teeth ', i.e. ' a row of teeth '.

l. 246. usum, ' power '.

ll. 247-249. He also invented the geometric compasses.

l. 247. et, ' also '.

l. 247. bracchia. We speak rather of the ' legs ' of a pair of compasses.

l. 248. aequali spatio distantibus illis, ' whilst they stood apart at an even distance '. distantibus illis is abl. abs., and illis refers to the bracchia of l. 247.

l. 249. **staret**, ' stood fast '.

l. 250. The **arx Minervae** at Athens stood on the Acropolis.

l. 251. **praecipitem** agrees with **eum**, the understood object of **misit**.

l. 251. **lapsum**, for (**eum**) **lapsum** (**esse**).

l. 252. **quae**. The relative refers to **Pallas**, later in the line.

l. 252. **ingeniis**, ' (men of) genius '.

l. 253. **medio in aëre**, i.e. before he could crash to death.

l. 255. **quod et ante**, ' even what (it was) before '. That is the name Perdix, which was his as a man, became that of the partridge.

l. 258. **propter**, usually ' on account of ', here means ' near'.

l. 260. **tellus Aetnaea**. ' The land of Etna ' is, of course, Sicily, to which island Ovid now brings Daedalus. Note the quantity of the final syllable of **tellūs**.

l. 261. **Daedalon**. **-on** is the acc. sg. ending in the Greek second declension.

l. 261. **supplice**. ' His suppliant ' is Daedalus, who had begged the protection of Cocalus against the pursuit of Minos.

l. 261. **Cocalus**, king of Camicus in Sicily.

l. 262. **mitis**, i.e. **quod arma sumpsit**. **habebatur**, ' was deemed ', a not uncommon meaning of **habeo** in the passive.

l. 263. **Thesea laude**, ' through the merit of Theseus ', abl. of cause. **Thesēā** is abl. sg. fem. of the adjective **Thesēŭs**, ' of Theseus '.

l. 265. **vocant**, ' they call upon '; ' they ' are the Athenians.

l. 265. **sanguine voto**. **voto** is perfect participle of **voveo** : ' that had been vowed '. Evidently victims had been vowed in the event of Theseus' enterprise proving successful.

l. 267. **sparserat**, ' had spread abroad '.

l. 268. **Theseos**. **-ōs** is a Greek genitive sing. termination.

l. 268. **populi**, nom. pl.

l. 268. **Achāĭă**, scanned as four syllables.

l. 268. **cepit**, ' contained ', ' embraced '.

l. 269. **huius**, i.e. ' Theseus '.

l. 269. **magnis periclis**, ' in their great peril ', pl. for sg. Probably abl. of cause, and literally ' because of . . .'

l. 270. **Calydon**, name of a town in Aetolia, Central Greece.

l. 270. **Meleagron**. For the ending see note on **Daedalon** l. 261.

l. 270. **haberet. quamvis** usually, though not always in Ovid, takes the subjunctive.

l. 271. **sollicita**. Scan the line.

l. 271. **supplex**. Translate as adv., ' humbly '.

l. 271. **petendi**, ' of their asking ', gerund.

l. 272. **Dianae**. The goddess was enraged (**infesta**) because Oeneus, king of Calydon and father of Meleager, in honouring the gods for an abundant harvest, had failed to include her.

l. 273. **Oenea**, Greek acc. sg., 3rd declension.

l. 273. **namque**. This is a strengthened form of **nam**.

l. 273. **ferunt**, ' they say ', a not uncommon meaning.

l. 273. **successibus**, abl. dependent on **pleni**.

l. 273. **anni**, gen., dependent on **primitias**.

l. 274. **sua** refers to **Lyaeo**, not, as it should, to **Oenea**.

l. 275. **Palladios latices**, ' the oil pressed from olives '. Pallas, or Minerva as the Romans called her, was protectress of the olive.

l. 275. **libasse**, for **libavisse**.

l. 276. **coeptus ab agricolis**, ' begun with the gods of tillage ' (*lit.* ' farmers '), i.e. the three gods just mentioned.

l. 276. **pervenit ad**, ' extended to '.

l. 277. **relictas cessasse**, ' were left and stood idle '. It has been pointed out before how frequently Latin prefers to use a participle in the place of the first of two finite verbs, or as here, of the first of two infinitives. cessasse = cessavisse.

l. 279. **impune,** ' without taking revenge '.

l. 279. **feremus.** Supply as object **hoc** =the slight.

l. 280. **quaeque** =et quae. **quae** is nom. pl. fem. of the relative pronoun, and refers to **nos,** the understood subject of **dicemur.** Diana is speaking of herself, though she uses the plural. With **quae** supply **dicimur** : ' and I, who (am called) unhonoured, shall not also be called unavenged '.

l. 281. **Oeneos.** See note on **Theseos,** l. 268.

l. 281. **spreta,** nom. sg. agreeing with the subject (Diana) of **inquit** : ' being (thus) slighted '.

l. 282. **aprum quanto,** etc. The relative **quanto** refers to an understood **tantum** in agreement with **aprum.** Lit., ' a boar (so great) as grassy Epirus has not bigger bulls, but the Sicilian fields have smaller (ones) '. **quanto** is abl. of comparison. The meaning, somewhat obscurely put, is ' a boar big as the bulls of grassy Epirus, and bigger than those of the Sicilian fields '.

l. 283. **Epiros,** nom. sg. fem., Greek 2nd declension.

l. 285. **rigidis hastilibus,** dat. after **similes.**

l. 288. **dentes,** ' tusks '.

l. 288. **aequantur,** deponent rather than passive, ' are as big as '.

l. 288. **Indis,** i.e. ' of elephants '. The elephant was often termed **Inda belua,** ' the Indian beast '.

l. 289. **frondes adflatibus ardent.** Its breath is so hot that it sets the trees ablaze.

ll. 290, 291. **modo . . . nunc,** for **modo . . . modo,** ' now . . . now '.

l. 291. **matura vota,** ' the full-grown hopes ' are of course the crops.

l. 291. **fleturi,** gen. sg. masc. fut. partic. of **fleo,** ' fated to weep '.

l. 292. **Cererem.** The name of the goddess is put for the produce of which she is protectress, ' grain ', ' corn '.

l. 292. **area frustra et frustra horrea,** ' in vain the threshing floor, in vain the barns '.

l. 294. **fetūs,** nom. pl., ' fruit ' (of the vine, as is made clear by **palmite**).

l. 296. **et,** ' too '. Notice the position of the word.

l. 296. **non . . . -ve . . . -ve . . . non,** ' neither . . . nor . . . nor '.

l. 298. **moenibus,** possibly an ablative of means, but we should say ' within the walls '.

l. 299. **donec,** i.e., the boar's ravages continued, ' until . . .'

l. 299. **Meleagros,** nom. sg.

l. 299. **unā,** adv., see note, l. 195.

l. 300. **coiere** = coiverunt.

l. 300. **cupidine,** abl. of cause, ' in their desire '.

l. 300. **laudis,** a good example of the objective genitive. See note on **loci,** l. 184.

There follows (ll. 301-323) a list of the iuvenes who accompanied Meleager.

l. 301. **Tyndaridae gemini.** ' The twin sons of Tyndareus ' are Castor and Pollux.

l. 301. **spectatus,** ' renowned '.

l. 301. **caestibus,** abl. of respect, but translate ' for his boxing '.

l. 301. **alter,** Pollux.

l. 302. **alter,** Castor.

l. 302. **equo,** see note on **caestibus,** l. 301, and translate ' for his horsemanship '.

l. 302. **primae ratis,** i.e. the Argo, in which Jason and his comrades sailed to win the Golden Fleece.

l. 303. **concordia,** ' partnership ', i.e. that of Theseus and

Pirithous. **concordia** is in apposition to **Theseus cum Pirithoo** = Theseus et Pirithous.

l. 304. The **Thestiadae** were Plexippus and Toxeus, mentioned by name later, ll. 440, 441.

l. 304. **proles**, in apposition to **Lynceus** and **Idas**.

l. 305. **iam non**, ' no longer '.

l. 305. **Caeneus**, originally a woman, had his sex changed at his own request by Neptune.

l. 307. **cretus Amyntore**, ' son of Amyntor ', lit. ' sprung from A.'. **Amyntore** is abl. of origin.

l. 308. **pares**, ' equal ', i.e. ' twin '. ' The sons of Actor ' were named Eurytus and Cleatus.

l. 309. **nec Telamon aberat.** A way of saying ' Telamon, too, was there '.

l. 309. **creator Achillis**, i.e. Peleus.

l. 310. **Pheretiade** = Admetus.

Note the scansion of this line :

cūmquĕ Phĕ | rētĭă | dē ĕt Hў̆ | āntē | ō Ĭŏl | āŏ.

Observe that there are two cases of final vowels not elided before initial vowels, and two cases of long vowels immediately preceding other vowels within a word, whereas in Latin a vowel in this position is normally short. Such irregularities are not unusual in a line, consisting largely, as this does, of Greek proper names.

l. 311. **cursu**, abl. of respect, ' in running '.

l. 313. **primis etiamnum Nestor in annis.** Nestor, here still a young man, appears in Homer as the aged counsellor of the Greek heroes in the Trojan War.

l. 314. **quos** = (ei) quos. The sons of Hippocoon are meant.

l. 315. **Penelopes**, Greek gen. sg., 1st declension.

l. 315. **socer**, i.e. Laertes.

l. 316. **Ampycides.** ' The son of Ampyx ' is Mopsus, famous as a prophet.

l. 316. **adhuc a coniuge tutus.** ' The son of Oecleus ',

Amphiaraus, was persuaded by his wife to join in an attack on Thebes in which it had been prophesied that he would perish.

l. 317. **Tegeaea,** ' she of Tegea ', is Atalanta, who as a famous huntress is not out of place in this company of heroes.

l. 317. **decus** is in apposition to **Tegeaea.**

l. 318. **huic,** ' her '. It is very common to find in Latin a dative where we should expect a possessive genitive.

l. 318. **mordebat,** ' bit ', i.e. ' pinned '.

l. 320. **resonabat,** ' rattled '. Her quiver (poetically described as **custos telorum,** with **custos** taking the gender of **pharetra,** ' quiver '), or rather the arrows in it, rattled as she walked.

l. 321. **laeva,** sc. **manus.**

l. 322. **cultu,** abl. of respect, ' in dress '.

l. 322. **quam** = (ea) **quam,** ' that which ' = ' such as '.

l. 322. **dicere vere posses,** ' one could truthfully call '. The second person singular of the subjunctive is used in Latin where we use ' one ' or ' you ' and the French ' *on* '. It is called the subjunctive of the ideal (i.e. not real) second person.

l. 324. **pariter vidit, pariter optavit** = simulac (as soon as) **vidit, optavit.**

l. 325. **renuente deo,** ' against the will of heaven ', abl. abs. **deus** is often used in this general sense.

l. 325. **flammas,** of love.

l. 326. **hausit,** ' conceived '.

l. 326. **O felix, siquem, etc.** Lit. ' O happy, if she shall deem any man worthy (as) husband ', i.e. ' Happy the man, if such there be, whom she shall deem worthy of herself as husband '.

l. 327. **sinit,** singular verb, though there are two subjects, **tempus** and **pudor.** Supply **eum** as object.

l. 328. **magni certaminis,** i.e. the struggle with the boar.

certaminis is gen. of definition, as that genitive is called which takes the place of simple apposition. Cf. City *of London*.

l. 329. **trabibus**, usually 'beams', or 'planks', here 'trees'.

l. 330. **incipit a plano**, ' begins from the flat ', i.e. ' slopes upward from a plain '.

l. 331. **quo**, adv., 'to this'.

l. 331. **pars tendunt. pars,** being equal to **nonnulli,** ' some ', here takes a plural verb, as it often does. This is an example of **constructio ad sensum**, ' construction according to the sense ', rather than in accordance with the rules of grammar. Similarly in the following line.

l. 332. **canibus**, dat. Such a dative is commonly found with compound verbs meaning ' to take away ', and is called dative of advantage or disadvantage according to the sense.

l. 333. **pedum**, i.e. the boar's feet.

l. 333. **suum periclum**, i.e. ' what will but imperil them '.

l. 334. **quo**, adv., ' into which '.

l. 334. **se demittere**, ' to let themselves down ', i.e. ' to fall '.

l. 335. **adsuerant**=**adsueverant**.

l. 335. **tenet**, sg. verb with five subjects. Translate ' possess ', i.e. ' occupy '.

l. 335. **ima**, ' the lowest (parts) ', i.e. ' the bottom '.

l. 335. **lacunae**=**vallis** above, ' the hollow '; gen. dependent on **ima**.

l. 336. **lenta** with **salix** probably.

l. 337. **sub**, ' under ', i.e. ' overshadowed by '.

l. 337. **harundine**, sg. for pl.

l. 338. **hinc**, with **excitus**, ' roused from this (covert) '.

l. 338. **violentus.** Translate as adv.

l. 339. **fertur**, ' rushes ', a common meaning of **feror**, which is almost a deponent here.

l. 339. **ut,** etc., i.e. like lightning.

l. 339. **excussis,** ' shaken '.

l. 340. **incursu,** of the boar, of course.

l. 341. **dat,** ' gives out '.

l. 341. **praetenta tenent,** ' hold stretched out '.

l. 342. **dextra,** sc. **manu.**

l. 342. **tela lato vibrantia ferro,** ' their quivering, broad-bladed spears '. **lato ferro** is abl. of description.

l. 343. **ille,** i.e. the boar.

l. 343. **ut quisque furenti obstat,** ' as each (dog) stands in the way (of him) raging ', i.e. ' as each in turn seeks to bar his furious passage '. **furenti** is dative in agreement with **ei** understood, which depends on **obstat.**

l. 344. **latrantes** agrees with **eos** (=**canes**) understood.

l. 344. **ictu,** i.e. of its tusks.

l. 345. **Echionio lacerto,** ' by the arm of Echion '. Notice how adjectives can be formed from proper names, thus giving a metrical alternative to genitives. **Echionius = Echionis.**

l. 346. **vana fuit,** i.e. ' missed its mark '.

l. 346. **dedit,** ' dealt '.

ll. 347, 348. ' The next (spear), if it had not received its thrower's excessive strength, seemed likely-to-stick (**haesura**) in the back at-which-it-was-aimed (**petito**) '. **proxima** agrees with **cuspis** understood.

l. 347. **mittentis.** The present participle is here used as a noun. **usa foret. foret** =**esset,** and **utor** is here employed in an extended meaning which is however not uncommon. Notice in connection with **petito** how the perfect participle passive neatly takes the place of a relative clause.

l. 349. **longius,** ' too far ', a common meaning of the comparative.

l. 349. **auctor,** ' the thrower '. The word is subject to **erat** understood.

l. 349. **Pagasaeus.** Jason is so called because his famous ship, the Argo, sailed from Pagasae, in Thessaly.

l. 350. **Phoebe,** voc. of **Phoebus.**

l. 350. **Ampycides.** See note, l. 316.

l. 351. **da mihi contingere,** ' give me to hit ', i.e. ' grant that I may hit '.

l. 351. **quod petitur,** ' (that) which is aimed at ', i.e. ' the mark at which I aim '.

l. 352. **qua,** ' as far as '. Plainly one god could not thwart the wishes of another, and so Diana's boar, though struck, is unwounded.

l. 352. **illo** = Ampycide.

l. 353. **volanti iaculo,** see note on **canibus,** l. 332.

l. 355. **nec fulmine lenius,** ' not more mildly than a thunderbolt ', i.e. ' as fiercely as a thunderbolt '.

l. 357. **moles,** ' mass ', i.e. of stone. The simile is drawn from the **tormenta,** ' artillery ', of the Roman armies.

l. 357. **adducto concita nervo,** ' sped by the tautened string '.

l. 358. **milite,** sg. for pl.

l. 359. **sus.** It is unusual to end a hexameter with a monosyllable.

l. 360. **fertur.** See note on this word, l. 339.

l. 360. **Pelagona,** Greek acc. sg.

l. 360. **dextra cornua,** pl. for sg., ' the right wing ', i.e. of the line of hunters.

l. 360. **tuentes.** Make sure of this word. It has nothing to do with the French *tuer.*

l. 361. **iacentes,** ' as they lay '. The participle agrees with **eos** understood.

l. 362. **effugit.** Scan the line to determine whether the word is pres. or perf. (**effŭgit** or **effūgit**).

l. 362. **ictus,** acc. pl.

l. 363. **Hippocoonte,** abl. of origin.

l. 363. **trepidantem . . . nervi.** ' Trembling and preparing to turn his back, his sinews failed (him), his leg muscle being

G

torn '. The poples is the part behind the knee. The meaning is that a blow of the sharp tusk cut the leg muscles by
which he might have escaped. trepidantem and parantem
agree with eum understood, object of liquerunt.

l. 365. Pylius, i.e. Nestor, king of Pylos.

l. 365. citra, ' on this side of ', i.e. ' before '.

l. 365. perisset = periisset. forsitan, ' perhaps ', is followed
by the subjunctive.

l. 366. ' But taking his effort from his spear placed (in
the ground) ', i.e. ' using his spear, planted in the ground,
to give himself an impetus '. In other words Nestor gained
the safety of the tree by executing a form of pole-vault.

l. 367. ramis, dat. after insiluit.

l. 368. quem refers to hostem.

l. 369. tritis. terere here = ' to whet '.

l. 370. exitio, dative with imminet, ' is bent upon '.

l. 370. recentibus, ' freshly sharpened '.

l. 370. armis, i.e. the tusks, abl. with fidens. fido takes
dative of the person, but ablative of the thing, trusted in.

l. 371. Eurytidae. The son of Eurytus was called Hippasus.

l. 372. at gemini, etc., i.e. Castor and Pollux, the Tyndaridae of l. 301. nondum caelestia sidera. After their life
on earth the brothers became stars and served as a guide to
mariners.

l. 373. nive, abl. of comparison.

ll. 374, 375. ambo vibrata . . . spicula motu. ' Both bran-
dished with a quivering movement their pointed lances (lit.
points of their lances) hurled through the air ' (i.e. ' and
hurled them through the air '). It would be more natural
to have quassata vibrant, since the brandishing of course
preceded the throwing.

l. 376. fecissent, subjunctive in the apodosis of a condi-

tional sentence, ' they would have inflicted '. The verb of
the protasis is **isset** (=**iisset**), l. 377.

l. 376. **saetiger,** ' the bristle-bearer ', i.e. ' the boar '.

l. 377. **iaculis, equo,** datives dependent on **pervia. loca
pervia** is in apposition to **silvas.**

l. 378. **studioque incautus eundi,** ' unwary in his eagerness
to advance '. **studio** is abl. of cause, and **eundi,** lit. ' of
going ', is objective genitive dependent on **studio.**

l. 379. The addition of **ab** to the ablative of the instrument, **radice,** is poetic.

l. 380. **hunc** = Telamona.

l. 381. **nervo,** dat. after the compound verb **imposuit** which
has **sagittam** as its direct object.

l. 382. **fixa destringit.** Here the use of participle and main
verb is similar to that noted in ll. 374, 375, for the ' grazing '
(**destringit**) must have preceded the ' sticking fast ' (**fixa**).
Translated ' grazes and sticks fast '.

l. 382. **summum corpus,** possibly ' top of the body '. i.e.
' the back ', but more probably ' surface of the body ', i.e.
' the skin '.

l. 384. **successu,** abl. of cause with **laetior,** ' at the success '.

l. 384. **ictus,** gen. sg.

l. 386. **visum** goes in grammar with **cruorem.** Translate,
' having seen it '.

l. 388. **erubuere,** ' blushed ', with shame, that is, that the
boar should have been first wounded by a woman.

l. 389. **addunt animos,** ' inspire fresh courage '.

l. 390. ' Their number hampers the rain of shafts, and
frustrates the blows which they seek (to inflict) '. **turba**
may refer either to the throng of hunters or to the number
of weapons. In any case iactis, dative after **nocet,** agrees
with **telis** understood.

l. 391. **furens contra sua fata,** apparently ' burning to meet his doom '. It is implied that his destruction, which of course he did not foresee, was hastened by his eagerness.

l. 391. **Arcas,** i.e. Ancaeus.

l. 392. **femineis** (sc. telis), dat. dependent on **praestent,** ' excel '.

l. 392. **quid,** ' how much ', acc. of extent. Cf. note on ecquid, l. 131.

l. 392. **praestent,** subjunctive in an indirect question.

l. 393. **operique meo concedite,** ' give way to my work ', i.e. ' leave this task to me '.

l. 394. **licet,** conjunction =' although ', followed as usual by the subjunctive.

l. 394. **hunc,** i.e. the boar.

l. 394. **Latonia.** ' The daughter of Latona ' is Diana.

l. 395. **invita Diana,** abl. abs., ' with Diana unwilling ', i.e. ' against Diana's will '.

l. 396. **tumidus,** translate as an adverb.

l. 397. **manu utraque. uterque,** ' each of two ' is often best translated ' both '.

l. 398. **digitis,** ' toes ', dat. after the compound verb **in-stiterat.**

l. 398. **pronos suspensus in ictus,** ' poised for a downward stroke '. **ictus,** pl. for sg.

l. 399. **audentem,** lit. ' (him) daring ', i.e. ' his reckless foe '.

l. 399. **quaque,** ' and where '. This clause explains **summa inguina** in l. 400 and should be translated after it.

l. 400. **summa inguina,** ' the upper groin '.

l. 401. **sanguine multo,** ' with a torrent of blood '.

l. 402. **lapsa fluunt,** ' come tumbling out '.

l. 403. **in adversum hostem,** lit. ' against the confronting foe ', i.e. ' against the foe before him '.

l. 404. **valida.** Scan the line to determine the quantity of the final syllable. Only by so doing can you say whether valida goes with venabula or with dextra.

l. 405. **procul,** with consiste.

l. 405. **Aegides.** ' The son of Aegeus ' is Theseus.

l. 406. **pars,** ' half '.

l. 406. **licet eminus esse fortibus.** Supply nobis (dat.), with which fortibus agrees. ' We can be brave and yet stand aloof '. Remember that the impersonal verb licet takes the dative.

l. 407. **Ancaeo nocuit,** ' was A.'s undoing '.

l. 408. **cornum.** Spear shafts were often made of cornel wood. Translate ' cornel-wood shaft '.

l. 408. **aerata cuspide,** abl. of description or quality, always consisting, remember, of noun *and adjective*.

l. 409. **quo . . . librato . . . futuro.** Translate this double ablative absolute by two ' though ' clauses, and quo, referring to cornum, by ' this '.

l. 409. **votique potente futuro,** ' and seemed about to be successful '. For voti potens see note on l. 56, and cf. l. 80.

l. 411. **Aesonides,** i.e. Jason.

l. 411. **ab illo,** ' away from him ', i.e. the boar.

l. 412. **in immeriti fatum latrantis,** ' to the destruction of an undeserving barker ', i.e. ' of an innocent dog '.

l. 413. **coniectum fixum est.** The participle coniectum and the verb fixum est have as subject a nominative quod, to be understood from the accusative quod of l. 411. The change of subject is awkward.

l. 413. **tellure,** local abl. without preposition, ' in the earth '.

l. 414. **manus,** translate here, ' aim '.

l. 414. **Oenidae,** ' of the son of Oeneus ', i.e. Meleager.

l. 414. **variat,** ' changes '.

l. 414. **missis duabus,** abl. abs.

l. 415. **terra, tergo.** See note on, and translation of **tellure**, l. 413.

l. 415. **tergo,** the boar's back, of course.

l. 416. **nec mora (est),** ' nor is there delay ', i.e. ' at once '.

l. 416. **corpora versat in orbem,** ' whirls his body round in circles '.

l. 418. **vulneris auctor,** ' he who inflicted the wound '.

l. 419. **adversos in armos,** ' in the shoulder turned towards him '. **armos,** pl. for sg.

l. 420. **clamore secundo,** ' with favourable shouting ', i.e. ' with shouts of victory '.

l. 421. **petunt.** The object is **coniungere,** ' seek to clasp (lit. join) his victorious right hand in their own '.

l. 422. **multa tellure iacentem,** ' lying on much earth ', i.e. ' covering so much ground '.

ll. 423, 424. **tutum esse putant,** ' think that (it) is safe '.

l. 425. **ipse,** i.e. Meleager.

l. 426. **sume . . . iuris,** ' take the spoil that is of my right ', i.e. ' rightly mine '.

l. 426. **Nonacria** = Atalanta, who dwelt near Nonacris, a town in Arcadia.

l. 427. **in partem veniat mea gloria tecum,** ' let my glory come into share with thee ', i.e. ' be shared with thee '. What use of the subjunctive is **veniat?**

l. 429. **terga,** probably = ' skin ' here.

l. 429. **ora,** ' head '.

l. 430. ' The author of the gift is for a delight to her along with the gift ', i.e. ' she delights no less in the giver than in the gift itself.

l. 431. **invidere** = inviderunt.

l. 431. **toto agmine,** ' in all (i.e. throughout) the company'.

l. 432. **e quibus,** ' out of these '.

l. 432. **ingenti voce,** abl. of manner with **clamant,** l. **434.**

l. 433. **pone,** ' put (them) down '. **pono** often has **this** meaning.

l. 433. **age** is often used with another imperative much **as** we use ' come '.

l. 433. **nec intercipe.** An imperative is sometimes found in poetry with a negative. In prose we should have **neve interceperis** (perf. subj.).

l. 434. **Thestiadae.** See note on l. 304.

l. 434. **fiducia formae,** ' trust in thy beauty '. **formae** is a good example of the objective genitive, explained in the note on **loci,** l. 184.

l. 435. **decipiat, sit.** For the subjunctives cf. the translation of **veniat,** l. 427.

l. 435. **sit longe tibi,** ' be far from thee ', i.e. ' avail not to protect thee '. **tibi,** which we must render ' *from* thee ', is dative of disadvantage.

l. 436. **auctor,** sc. **muneris,** ' the giver '.

l. 436. **huic** and **illi,** see note on, and translation of, **tibi,** l. 435. **huic** (fem.) is Atalanta, **illi** Meleager.

l. 436. **ius muneris,** ' the right of (bestowing) the **gift** '.

l. 437. **non tulit,** ' endured (this) not '.

l. 437. **Mavortius,** ' son of Mars ' =Meleager. There seems to have been some doubt as to his parentage, as in l. 414 he is called Oenides, ' son of Oeneus '.

l. 439. **facta minis quantum distent,** ' how much deeds differ from threats '. **distent** is subjunctive in an indirect question.

l. 440. **nil tale timentia,** ' fearing nothing such ', i.e. ' dreading no such doom '. We should expect the phrase to qualify **Plexippi** rather than **pectora.**

l. 441. **Toxea,** acc. sg. of **Toxeus.**

l. 441. **quid faciat,** indirect deliberative question dependent on **dubium,** ' uncertain what to do '.

l. 443. **patitur.** The subject is **Meleager,** the object **Toxea.**

l. 443. **calidum prioris caede,** ' warm from the blood of his first (victim) '. **caede** is abl. of cause, and **calidum** agrees with **telum.**

l. 444. **consorti sanguine,** abl. of means with **recalfecit.**

l. 445. **deum,** gen. pl.

l. 445. **templis,** dat. of motion towards with **ferebat,** instead of the usual **ad templa.**

l. 445. **nato victore,** ' her son (being) victor ', abl. abs., i.e. ' in honour of her son's victory '. **nato,** of course, refers to **Meleager.**

l. 446. **fratres.** Plexippus and Toxeus were thus Meleager's uncles.

l. 447. **quae,** ' she ', i.e. Althaea.

l. 447. **plangore dato,** ' a wail having been given ', i.e. ' having given vent to a wail '.

l. 448. **et auratis,** etc., ' changed black (garments) with golden garments ', i.e. ' changed her golden robes for black '.

l. 449. **est editus,** ' was reported '.

l. 450. **in poenae amorem,** ' into a desire for vengeance '. **poenae** is objective genitive.

l. 451. **partus** (acc. pl.) **enixa,** ' having brought forth her offspring '.

l. 452. **Thestias.** ' The daughter of Thestius ' is Althaea.

l. 452. **triplices sorores.** ' The three sisters ' are the Parcae or Fates, who spin the thread of human destiny. **triplices** is used by poetic licence for **tres.**

l. 453. **impresso pollice,** ' with thumb pressed on ', i.e. ' with firm pressure of their thumbs '.

l. 454. **tempora eadem,** ' the same span (of life) '.

l. 454. **ligno,** i.e. the stipes mentioned in l. 451.

l. 455. **quo carmine dicto,** abl. abs.

l. 458. **penetralibus imis,** ' in the very depths of the house '. The word **penetralia** is usually found, as here, in the plural and means ' the inmost parts '.

l. 459. **servatus.** The participle does the work of a causal clause, ' because (so) preserved '.

l. 460. **hunc** =torrem.

l. 460. **poni,** ' to be laid in position '. The passive infinitive is sometimes found after **impero,** instead of the normal **ut** clause.

l. 461. **positis,** dat., ' and *when they were laid* brings cruel flames near *them* '.

l. 462. **flammis,** dative after the compound verb **imponere.**

l. 463. **coepta quater tenuit,** ' four times checked her beginnings ', i.e. ' four times stayed her hand '.

l. 463. **pugnant,** ' war within her '.

l. 464. **duo diversa nomina.** Presumably **filius** and **frater.**

l. 464. **trahunt,** ' distract '.

l. 465. **metu,** ' in dread ', abl. of cause with **pallebant.**

l. 465. **sceleris futuri,** ' of her projected crime '.

l. 465. **ora,** pl. for sg.

ll. 467, 468. ' And now her face was like (that of) one threatening some cruel deed (*lit.* something cruel), now one which you could believe had pity '.

l. 467. **minanti,** dat. after **similis,** is put for **vultus minantis.**

l. 468. **quem** for ei (**vultui**) **quem.**

l. 468. **posses,** potential subjunctive.

l. 469. **cum siccaverat. cum** with the perfect and pluperfect indicative means ' whenever '.

l. 470. **utque carina** introduces a simile.

l. 471. **ventoque contrarius aestus,** ' and tide at war with wind '. **vento** is dative dependent on **contrarius.**

l. 472. **incerta,** adjective put for adverb, ' uncertainly '.

l. 473. **Thestias,** see note, l. 452.

l. 473. **haud aliter,** ' not otherwise ' =' even so '.

l. 473. **dubiis adfectibus errat,** ' wavers under conflicting emotions '. **adfectibus** is abl. of cause.

l. 475. **parente**, abl. of comparison.

l. 476. **leniat**, final subjunctive.

l. 477. **impietate pia est**, ' she is in lack of duty dutiful '. She is **pia** in avenging her brother, but shows **impietas** in destroying the stipes on which her son's life depends. This figure of speech, in which an apparently absurd contradiction reveals, upon examination, a pointed truth, is called oxymoron, a Greek word meaning ' pointedly foolish '. A favourite example from English literature is the following, from Tennyson :

' His honour rooted in dishonour stood,
    And faith unfaithful kept him falsely true '.

l. 478. **cremet**, jussive subjunctive, ' let that pyre consume,' etc.

l. 478. **mea viscera**, ' my flesh ', because born of her body.

l. 480. **infelix**, ' the unhappy (creature) '.

l. 481. **triplices**, see note on this, l. 452.

l. 482. **Eumenides**, the Greek name for the Furiae, or Furies. The word means literally ' the kindly ones ', and was given by the Greeks in the hope of propitiating them, much as the mischievous fairies of our own countryside were called ' the good people '.

l. 482. **sacris furialibus**, ' to a sacrifice pleasing-to-the-Furies '.

l. 483. **pianda est**, gerundive with the verb **sum**, expressing obligation, ' must be atoned '. Similarly **addendum** in l. 484.

l. 485. **pereat**, jussive, cf. translation of **cremet**, l. 478.

l. 486. **an** sometimes introduces an indignant rhetorical question, ' shall Oeneus enjoy? ' (*rhetorical*, because carrying its own answer, ' no ').

l. 488. **animae recentes**, ' new-made spirits '.

l. 489. **magno**, abl. of price, ' at great cost '.

l. 490. **pignora**, in apposition to **inferias**, and pl. for sg. The word **pignus**, meaning usually ' pledge ', occurs often, in poetry, in the sense ' a pledge of love ', i.e. ' a child '. In this case, of course, Meleager is meant.

l. 491. **ei,** interjection.

l. 491. **quo,** adv.

l. 491. **matri,** ' *a* mother '.

l. 492. **deficiunt,** ' lack the strength '.

l. 492. **fatemur,** pl. for sg.

l. 493. **cur pereat,** for the usual **ut pereat,** depends on **meruisse.** Translate ' to die '.

l. 493. **mortis mihi displicet auctor,** ' the agent of death is displeasing to me '. She means ' the *rôle of* agent '. Translate : ' but I am loth to be the agent of his death '.

l. 494. **impune feret,** ' shall he carry (it) off without punishment ', i.e. ' shall he go unscathed '.

l. 496. **cinis exiguus gelidaeque umbrae,** ' a handful of ashes and shivering ghosts '. (Miller : Loeb Translation.)

l. 498. **trahat,** ' bring down with him '.

l. 498. **patriaeque ruinam,** ' and his fatherland in ruin ', lit. ' the ruin of his fatherland ' which is ill joined as an object with **spem** and **regnum.**

l. 500. The order for translation is **et labores bis quinque mensum** (for **mensium) quos sustinui.**

l. 501. **primis ignibus.** ' The first fire ' is that on which the Parcae placed the faggot, and from which Althaea snatched it.

l. 501. **utinam arsisses,** ' would thou hadst burned '. **arsisses** is optative subjunctive, i.e. the subjunctive used to express a wish. The pluperfect tense is used for wishes impossible of fulfilment, the event having already determined otherwise. With the optative subjunctive **utinam** is frequently found.

l. 501. **infans,** ' (as) a babe '. Notice that ' as ' often has to be supplied in such cases of apposition.

l. 502. **id,** i.e. the burning of the brand.

l. 502. **munere,** ' favour '.

l. 503. **moriere,** parse carefully.

l. 503. **cape.** Althaea is still addressing Meleager.

l. 504. **mox stipite rapto,** ' then (**mox**) by my snatching of the brand ', lit. ' by the brand having been snatched '. Notice once again this use of the participle where English would use a verbal noun.

l. 505. **vel me,** etc., ' or bury me with my brothers ', lit. ' add me to my brothers' tombs '.

l. 506. **quid agam?** ' what am I to do ? ' For the subjunctive (deliberative), see note on **requiram,** l. 232.

l. 506. **modo** is answered by **nunc** in l. 508, instead of by a second **modo :** ' now . . . now '.

l. 507. **ante oculos mihi sunt,** ' are to me before the eyes ', a way of saying ' are before my eyes '.

l. 507. **tantae,** rather ' so impious ' than ' so great '.

l. 508. **nomina,** pl. for sg.

l. 509. **me miseram !** ' ah, wretched me ! ' The accusative is called that of *exclamation.*

ll. 510, 511. The order is **dummodo ipsa sequar solacia quae dedero vobis, vosque.** The **solacia** (pl. for sg.) is of course the destruction of her son by the burning of the brand.

l. 511. **sequar. dummodo,** ' provided that ', regularly takes the subjunctive.

l. 511. Scan to determine the quantities of the final syllables of **dextra** and **aversa.**

ll. 513, 514. The order is **stipes ille aut dedit, aut visus est dedisse, gemitūs.**

l. 514. **ut,** with indic., always ' as ' or ' when '.

l. 514. **ab.** The preposition is irregular in the case of the abl. of the instrument, but the use is helped out here by the poet's conceit that the flames were sentient, as **invitis** shows. Note the similar use of the preposition in l. 515.

l. 515. **inscius atque absens.** Meleager has not yet returned from the hunt.

l. 516. **caecis.** caecus, properly ' unseeing ', ' blind ', is very frequent in the meaning ' unseen '.

l. 518. **cadat.** The subjunctive is of virtual Oratio Obliqua, that is, the cadat represents the cado of Meleager's own thought. The clause **quod cadat,** etc., depends on **maeret.**

l. 518. **leto,** abl. of cause, qualified by **ignavo** and **sine sanguine** (' bloodless '). As a warrior and hunter he would have preferred death in battle or the chase.

l. 519. **felicia,** because Ancaeus had met the death Meleager envied, l. 401.

l. 519. **dicit,** ' calls '.

l. 521. **sociam tori,** i.e. his wife, named Cleopatra.

l. 521. **ore,** ' utterance '.

l. 522. **ignis,** the fire, that is, that consumes the brand.

l. 524. **leves,** ' thin '.

l. 525. **prunam,** the glowing wood of the brand.

l. 526. **iacet,** ' lies low ', ' is brought low '. **Alta,** possibly ' haughty ' rather than ' high '.

l. 527. **scissae capillos.** Latin poets frequently construct a passive verb with the accusative case. It is possible to explain the present case as an imitation of the Greek *middle* voice, which, having forms largely identical with the passive, denotes doing something *to* or *for oneself.* Translate ' with torn tresses '.

l. 528. **planguntur.** The passive here is equivalent to **plangunt se,** ' beat themselves ', i.e. ' their breasts ', the usual manifestation of mourning among women in ancient times.

l. 528. **Eveninae,** ' daughters of Evenus ', i.e. the women of Calydon, since the Evenus was the river on which that town stood.

l. 530. **humi fusus,** ' outstretched upon the earth '. **fusus,** lit. ' poured ', well suggests the abandonment of his grief.

l. 530. **increpat,** because he had lived to see not only the death of his son, but also of his wife, as ll. 531-2 explain.

l. 531. **de matre,** ' as for the mother '.

l. 531. **sibi** goes closely with **conscia,** ' aware within itself '.

l. 533. **deus,** general, ' heaven '.

l. 533. **sonantia linguis,** ' sounding with tongues ', where we should say ' with speaking tongues '.

l. 534. **Helicona,** acc. sg. of a Greek noun. Helicon, a mountain in Bœotia, was the fabled home of Apollo and the Muses, patrons of poetry. Thus the meaning of **totum Helicona** is ' completest inspiration '.

l. 534. **dedisset,** ' had given ', the usual mood and tense for a supposition contrary to the fact in past time. It is balanced by the imperfect **persequerer,** ' could I report ', this tense being used for similar suppositions relating to present time.

l. 535. **sororum,** i.e. of Meleager.

l. 536. **liventia,** lit. ' black and blue ', is used proleptically, i.e. it expresses the *effect* of the action denoted by the verb **tundunt.** Translate **liventia tundunt,** ' bruise with beating '.

l. 537. **manet,** i.e. before it is consumed in the pyre.

l. 537. **refoventque foventque,** ' fondle again and again '.

l. 538. **ipsi,** dat. = corpori.

l. 538. **posito,** ' when it was placed on the pyre '.

l. 539. **post cinerem,** ' after (it was turned to) ashes '.

l. 540. **adfusae,** see note on fusus, l. 530. **tumulo,** dat., goes with it.

l. 540. **signataque saxo nomina complexae,** ' embracing the name marked upon the stone ', or as we should put it, ' embracing the stone inscribed with his name '.

l. 542. **quas** is object of **adlevat,** l. 545, and refers to the sisters of Meleager.

l. 542. **Parthaoniae,** with **domŭs** (gen.), l. 543. Parthaon was the father of Oeneus, grandfather of Meleager.

l. 542. **Latonia** = Diana.

l. 542. **clade** depends on **exsatiata,** which agrees with **Latonia.**

l. 543. **praeter Gorgen,** etc. Two of Meleager's sisters, being already wives and therefore absent from Calydon, escaped the metamorphosis of the rest.

l. 543. **Gorgen,** acc. sg.

l. 543. **nurumque,** etc. ' The daughter-in-law of high-born Alcmena ' is Deianira, wife of Hercules.

l. 544. **natis pennis,** abl. abs., ' feathers having been born ', i.e. ' having caused feathers to sprout '.

l. 545. **per,** ' along '.

l. 546. **corneaque ora facit,** ' makes their mouths horny ', i.e. ' changes their mouths to beaks '.

l. 546. **versas,** ' (thus) transfigured '. The sisters of Meleager became guinea-hens, known as Meleagrides.

l. 547. **parte,** ' his share '. The word depends on **functus,** from **fungor,** which governs the abl.

l. 548. **Erechtheas,** ' Athenian ', because Erechtheus was an ancient king of Athens. Remember what has been said about the allusiveness of Latin epithets.

l. 548. **Tritonidos,** gen. sg.

ll. 548, 549. **arces, moras,** pl. for sg.

l. 549. **fecit,** ' caused '.

l. 549. **Achelous,** god of the Greek river of that name.

l. 549. **eunti** agrees with **ei** (= Theseo) understood, and is dative of disadvantage. Translate ' as he went '.

l. 551. **Cecropida,** Greek voc. sg., ' son of Cecrops '. Cecrops was the founder of Athens, and an ancestor, not the father, of Theseus.

l. 551. **nec committe,** cf. note on l. 433.

l. 552. **obliqua,** ' slantwise ', predicatively with **saxa.**

l. 553. **solent.** The subject is **undae,** understood from **undis,** l. 551.

l. 553. **ripae,** dat., dependent on **contermina.**

l. 554. **alta,** ' high-walled '.

l. 554. **trahi,** ' carried away '.

l. 554. **fortibus,** and **velocibus,** in l. 555, are predicates of **armentis** and **equis** respectively : ' nor did it then profit oxen to be strong, or horses to be swift '.

l. 556. **nivibus solutis,** abl. abs. Translate by a ' when ' clause.

l. 557. **vertice,** local abl.

l. 558. **dum,** ' until '. The subjunctive is final, as Theseus is exhorted to wait not merely ' until ' but ' in order that ' the river may subside.

l. 559. **tenues,** ' fallen '.

l. 559. **capiat,** ' contains '.

l. 559. **suus,** ' their own ', referring not, as usual, to the subject, but to the object.

l. 562. **pumice, tophis,** abls. of material depending on **structa,** ' built of '.

l. 562. **nec lēvibus.** Note the quantity. To call the tufa ' not smooth ' when ' rough ' is meant is a form of the figure of speech called *litotes*, literary understatement.

l. 564. **summa** sc. **atria,** i.e. the roof.

l. 564. **alterno murice,** ' with purple-shell alternate ', i.e. ' alternately with purple-shells '. The **murex** was the shell-fish from which the ancients obtained their purple dye.

l. 565. **Hyperione menso,** abl. abs. **menso** is from **metior.** Hyperion, a name for the sun-god. The gist of the line is that the day (**lux**) was two-thirds spent.

l. 566. **toris,** local abl.

l. 567. **hac (parte)...illa parte,** ' here ... there '. **Ixion-ides** and **Lelex** are two of the **comites,** with which word they are in apposition. ' The son of Ixion ' is Pirithous.

l. 568. **tempora,** acc. of respect, or of the part concerned, used in poetry to limit participles and adjectives : ' sprinkled as to the temples,' i.e., ' his temples sprinkled '.

l. 569. **quosque alios,** for aliique quos. The accusative **alios** is the result of ' attraction ' into the relative clause.

l. 569. **fuerat dignatus** = dignatus erat.

l. 570. **Amnis Acarnanum,** i.e. Achelous.

l. 570. **hospite tanto,** abl. of cause, ' at (entertaining) so great a guest ' (i.e. Theseus).

l. 571. **nudae vestigia,** ' bare as to the soles ', i.e. ' bare-footed '. For the acc. **vestigia** see note on **tempora,** l. 568.

l. 571. **adpositas instruxere epulis mensas,** ' brought up tables and laid them with the feast '. Notice how **adpositas** stands for **adposuerunt et,** a very common use of the participle.

l. 572. **dapibus remotis,** abl. abs. ; translate by a ' when ' clause.

l. 573. **in gemma,** lit. ' in a jewel ', poetic language for **in cyathis gemmatis,** ' in jewelled goblets '.

l. 573. **maximus heros,** i.e. Theseus.

l. 574. **oculis,** dat., dependent on the compound verb **subiecta.**

ll. 575, 576. The order is **doce nomen quod illa insula gerit.**

l. 576. **quamquam,** 'and yet '.

l. 576. **videtur.** The subject is **ea** (=insula) understood.

l. 577. The order is **(id) quod cernitis non est unum.**

l. 578. **discrimina,** ' the gaps (between them) '.

l. 579. **quoque minus** = et quo minus, ' and that ... the less '. **quo** is regularly used in place of **ut** in final clauses which contain a comparative.

l. 579. **mirere.** Parse carefully.

l. 580. **hae,** sc. insulae.

l. 580. **fuerant.** The pluperfect is equivalent to **erant olim,** ' were once '.

H

l. 582. **immemores nostri** is more important than the main verb **duxere**. Translate : ' (were) unmindful of me (as they) led the festal dance '.

l. 582. **nostri,** objective genitive ; **choreas,** pl. for sg.

l. 583. **quantusque feror . . . tantus eram,** ' and was as great as I flow (feror) when I flow fullest (plurimus) ', i.e. ' was as full as when my stream is at its fullest '. The passive of **fero** is often used as a deponent in the meaning ' go ', ' rush ', etc.

l. 584. **animis et undis,** ablatives of respect, dependent on **immanis,** ' terrible alike in anger and in flood '.

l. 586. **cum loco,** ' with the ground (they stood on) '.

l. 587. **fluctus nosterque marisque,** ' my flood and the sea's '.

l. 588. **resolvit** has as its object **eam** (=humum) understood.

l. 590. **recessit,** ' has withdrawn ', i.e. ' lies apart '.

l. 591. **Perimelen,** acc. sg., is in agreement with **eam,** object of **dicit,** understood.

l. 592. **huic dilectae,** ' from her, whom I loved '. The dative is one of disadvantage, usual after compound verbs meaning ' to take away '. Notice how the participle **dilectae** takes the place of a relative clause.

l. 593. **quod** =hoc.

l. 594. **periturae,** ' about to perish ', i.e. ' doomed '.

l. 595. **excepi.** Supply **eam** as object both of this verb and of **ferens.**

l. 596. **sortite,** voc. sg. masc. of the perf. partic. of the deponent **sortior** : ' thou who hast received as thy portion '.

l. 596. **Tridentifer,** ' bearer of the trident ', i.e. Neptune.

l. 601. **mersae,** ' to one drowned '.

l. 602. **vel sit locus ipsa licebit,** ' or it shall be permitted (that) she herself become a place ', i.e. ' or let her become a place herself '. **ut,** ' that ', is to be supplied, connecting **licebit** and **sit.** The conjunction is frequently omitted after **licet.**

l. 609. **loquor. dum,** meaning ' while ', is commonly used with the present tense, whatever the tense of the principal clause.

l. 609. **amplexa est,** etc., i.e. she was changed into land.

l. 610. ' and a solid island grew from her altered members '.

l. 611. **ab his** (*sc.* **verbis),** ' with these words '.

l. 612. **inridet.** The subject is **Ixione natus. credentes,** ' (them) believing ', i.e. ' their credulity '.

l. 612. **ut,** ' as '.

l. 613. **mentis,** gen. of respect, a use of the case confined to poetry and possibly derived from a similar use in Greek.

l. 613. **Ixione natus,** ' born from Ixion ' = ' son of Ixion ', i.e. Pirithous. **Ixione** is abl. of origin.

l. 615. **si dant.** We should expect si **credis dare,** ' if you think they give '.

l. 616. **probarunt** = **probaverunt.**

l. 617. **animo et aevo,** abls. of respect.

l. 618. **caeli,** ' of heaven ', i.e. ' of the gods '.

l. 620. **quoque minus dubites.** See note on a similar clause, l. 579.

l. 620. **tiliae,** dat. dependent on **contermina.**

l. 621. **collibus Phrygiis,** local abl. without prep.

l. 622. **Pelopeïa arva.** ' The lands of Pelops ' is an allusive way of saying Phrygia, of which country Pelops was king.

l. 623. **suo parenti,** dat. of the agent, to be translated ' by his own father '. This use of the case is not uncommon in poetry after the perf. partic. passive.

ll. 624, 625. **tellus olim, nunc undae.** The nouns are in apposition with **stagnum.**

l. 626. **Iuppiter.** Supply **venit** from the following line.

l. 626. **parente,** i.e. Jupiter.

l. 627. **Atlantiades caducifer,** i.e. Mercury, or Hermes, who was grandson of Atlas, and bearer of the Caduceus, or herald's staff. He was the messenger of the gods. Translate **caducifer** by ' herald '.

l. 627. **positis alis,** abl. abs.

l. 628. **locum requiemque,** ' a place *for* rest ', we should say.

l. 629. **una,** *sc.* **domus.**

l. 630. **tecta,** ' roofed '.

l. 631. **parili aetate,** abl. of description, always consisting of noun and adjective. Translate by an ' of ' phrase.

l. 632. **illa, illa.** Both the demonstratives go with **casā,** l. 633.

l. 632. **annis iuvenalibus,** abl. of time when.

ll. 633, 634. **fatendo, ferendo.** These gerunds are ablatives of means, and have **paupertatem** as their object.

l. 634. **levem** agrees with **eam** (=**paupertatem**) understood.

l. 634. **nec iniqua** =**et aequa,** cf. note on **nec levibus,** l. 562.

l. 635. **dominos,** etc. The interrogative particle **-ne,** which should introduce the first half of the indirect question, is transferred to the second half, replacing **an.** Translate as if the Latin were **dominosne illic an famulos requiras.**

l. 636. **duo, idem,** ' (they) two ', ' the same (two) '. **idem** is nom. pl. masc.

l. 637. **penates,** properly ' household gods ', is constantly used for ' home '.

l. 638. **intrarunt** =**intraverunt,** a syncopated form.

l. 638. **postes,** properly ' door posts ', is put for ' door '. This figure of speech is called *synecdoche.*

l. 639. **posito sedili,** abl. abs.

l. 640. **quo,** relative adv., referring to **sedili,** ' upon which '.

l. 643. **producit,** ' coaxed (it) '.

l. 644. **tecto,** abl. of place whence, going with **detulit:** ' from the roof '.

l. 645. **admovit.** The object is **ea** (=faces ramaliaque) understood.

l. 645. **aëno,** dat. after the compound verb **admovit.**

l. 646. **quodque = et quod.** **quod,** relative, refers to **holus** in l. 647. Take the first three words of l. 647, introducing them by the **-que,** before l. 646.

l. 647. **foliis,** ' of its leaves ', abl. of separation.

l. 648. **sordida, nigro.** The smoke that rose from the cottage fire made the beams ' black ', and the bacon ' dirty '.

l. 648. **terga,** pl. for sg.

l. 648. **suis,** gen. sg. of **sus.**

l. 649. **diu** goes with **servato.**

l. 649. **tergore.** Contrast this form (from a 3rd declension nominative **tergus**) with **terga** (l. 648) (from the more usual 2nd declension **tergum).**

l. 650. **sectamque = et cum (eam) secuisset.** Another instance of a participle standing for a complete clause.

l. 650. **domat,** ' proceeds to cook it '. **domo** is, literally, ' I tame '.

l. 651. **medias,** ' intervening ', i.e. between the putting on of the bacon to cook and its readiness for eating.

l. 655. **de,** ' from ', i.e. ' made of '.

l. 656. **lecto,** dat. after the compound verb **impositum.**

l. 656. **sponda pedibusque salignis.** **salignis** is to be taken with both nouns, which are ablatives of description qualifying **lecto,** ' placed upon a bed with frame and feet of willow-wood '.

l. 657. **nisi,** ' except '.

l. 657. **vestibus,** pl. for sg. It is called **vestis** (sg.) in l. 659.

l. 658. **consuerant = consueverant.**

l. 658. **et,** ' even '.

l. 659. **non indignanda,** ' not to be resented *by* ', i.e.
' a good match *for* '.

l. 660. **succincta,** ' girt up ', i.e. ' with her skirts tucked up '.

l. 661. **mensae,** etc.   The table was plainly three-legged.

l. 662. **testa.**   Scan to determine the quantity of the final
syllable.

l. 662. **parem** agrees with **eam** (=**mensam**) understood.

l. 662. **quae** =**ea,** standing for **testa.**

l. 663. **clivum sustulit.**   English prefers a pluperfect here,
' had removed (i.e. levelled) the slope '.

l. 663. **aequatam** agrees with **eam** (=**mensam**) understood.
Translate ' once it was levelled '.

l. 664. **hic,** adv., ' hereon '.

l. 664. **bicolor,** i.e. green and black.

l. 664. **sincerae,** ' pure ', i.e. ' maiden '.

l. 664. **baca,** that of the olive, of which Minerva was patro-
ness.   The olive is still a favourite among the *hors d'œuvre.*

l. 666. **lactis coacti,** ' of curdled milk ', i.e. cheese.

l. 667. **non acri favilla,** ' in the warm embers '.

l. 668. **omnia,** nom. in apposition to all the articles of food
mentioned.

l. 668. **fictilibus,** abl. of place, ' on earthenware '.

ll. 668, 669. **eodem argento,** abl. of description, ' of the
same fine material '.   A touch of humour, this, as the **crater,**
too, was **fictilis.**

l. 670. **qua cava sunt,** ' where they are hollow ', i.e. ' on
the inside '.

The phrase depends on **inlita** and should be taken after it.

l. 671. **epulasque.**   -**que** =' and (then) ', and **epulas** is the
main course of the meal, i.e. the **holus** and **terga suis** of ll.
647-8.

l. 671. **foci,** nom. pl. for sg.   **misere** (=**miserunt**) ' sent up '.

l. 672. nec = et non, the et introducing **vina referuntur**, and the **non** going closely with **longae**.

l. 672. **non longae senectae.** The wine, as befitted so humble a home, was ' of no long-stored vintage '.

l. 672. **referuntur**, ' brought back '. We are to understand that the same wine had previously been served with the **gustatio**, or *hors d'œuvre*.

l. 673. **paulum seducta**, qualifying **vina**, is to be taken before **dant**.

l. 673. **mensis secundis**, ' to the second course '.

l. 674. **hic, hic,** advbs., ' herein '.

l. 674. **nux, carica,** sg. for pl.

l. 674. **rugosis,** ' shrivelled ', i.e. ' dried '.

l. 677. **vultus,** of the old couple.

l. 678. **accessere,** simply ' there were '.

l. 678. **boni,** ' pleasant '.

l. 678. **nec** again = **et non**, as in l. 672. The **non** goes both with **iners** and **pauper.** Translate ' busy and generous goodwill '.

ll. 679, 680. The order is **interea vident cratera, totiens haustum, repleri sua sponte, vinaque** succrescere **per se.** The disguised gods are replenishing the wine miraculously.

l. 680. **vident,** subject Philemon and Baucis.

l. 680. **cratera,** acc. sg.

l. 683. **nullisque paratibus,** ' and for their no preparations ', i.e. ' their unreadiness '.

l. 684. **minimae,** ' tiny '.

l. 684. **custodia** = **custos,** abstract for concrete. In the well-known story of the Gallic assault on the Capitol, geese proved more vigilant sentinels than dogs.

l. 685. **domini,** ' the hosts '.

l. 686. **pennā,** abl. of respect with **celer,** ' swift of wing '.

l. 686. **tardos** agrees with **eos** (= Philemon and Baucis) understood.

l. 686. **aetate**, abl. of cause with **tardos**.

l. 688. **vetuere**. Supply as object **eum** (= anserem).

l. 689. **vicinia**, ' (this) neighbourhood '.

ll. 690, 691. **vobis . . . dabitur**. ' To you it shall be given to be exempt from this destruction (**mali**) '. The adjective **immunis** is generally followed by the genitive.

l. 692. **ardua**, neut. adj. used as a noun, ' the heights '.

l. 693. **levati**, ' supported (by), i.e. ' leaning (on) '.

l. 694. **longo clivo**, abl. of route, ' up the long slope '.

ll. 695, 696. **Tantum . . . potest**. The sense of this is that they were a bowshot from the summit.

l. 695. **summo**, neut. adj. used as noun. Cf. **ardua**, l. 692.

l. 695. **tantum, quantum**, accusatives of extent, telling *how far*.

l. 697. **cetera**, ' the rest (of the countryside) '.

l. 697. **tantum**, adv., ' only '.

l. 698. **suorum**, ' of their own (friends) '.

l. 699. **etiam** with **duobus dominis**, ' even for two occupants '.

l. 700. **furcas**. These are the forked wooden corner-posts of the hut.

l. 701. **stramina**, i.e. of the roof-thatch.

l. 701. **videntur**, ' appear '.

l. 703. **Saturnius**. ' The son of Saturn ' is Jupiter.

l. 704. **dicite**, supply **nobis**.

l. 704. **coniuge** is the regular abl. found with **dignus**.

l. 705. **optetis**, subjunctive in an indirect question.

l. 705. **cum . . . locutus**. The old couple conferred together.

l. 707. **esse**, governed by **poscimus**.

l. 708. **concordes**, nom.

l. 709. **auferat, videam, sim,** indirect petitions, dependent on **poscimus (ut).**

l. 709. **duos** agrees with **nos** understood.

l. 710. **sim tumulandus,** ' have to be buried '. The gerundive with **sum** expresses obligation, as usual.

l. 710. **ab illa.** The dative is normally used to express the agent with the gerundive of obligation.

l. 711. **tutela = tutores,** ' guardians ', abstract for concrete. Cf. **custodia** (=**custodes**), l. 684.

l. 712. **annis aevoque,** lit. ' with years and age ', i.e. ' with length of years '.

l. 712. **soluti,** ' worn out '.

l. 714. **casus,** ' fortunes ' acc. pl.

l. 714. **Philemona, Baucida,** accs. sg.

l. 715. **conspexit** has two separate subjects, **Baucis** and senior **Philemon,** and two object clauses (acc. + inf.) **Philemona frondere** and **Baucida frondere.** The sense is that each saw the other being turned into a tree.

l. 715. **senior,** sometimes, as here, means nc more than **senex.**

l. 716. The order is **iamque, cacumine crescente** (abl. abs.) **super geminos vultus, reddebant mutua dicta, dum licuit.**

l. 717. **reddebant mutua,** ' exchanged '.

l. 718. **simul, simul,** ' just as '.

l. 718. **abdita texit,** ' hid and covered '. As so often a participle and a finite verb express what English would prefer to do by means of two finite verbs.

l. 719. **de gemino corpore,** ' (sprung) from their two bodies ', lit. ' their twin body '.

l. 721. **non vani,** ' not frivolous ', i.e. ' grave ', ' responsible '.

l. 721. **neque erat cur vellent,** ' nor was there why they should wish, i.e. ' they had no cause to wish '. **vellent,** subjunctive in indirect question.

l. 723. **super.** We should say ' from '. The hanging of garlands at holy places was a form of worship among the ancients.

l. 723. **recentia,** ' fresh (ones) '.

l. 724. **cura,** complement of **sunt,** ' the good are a care unto the gods ', i.e. ' are cared for by the gods '.

l. 724. **qui,** supply as antecedent **ei,** subject to **coluntur.**

l. 725. **res,** ' the tale ' ; **auctor,** ' the teller '.

l. 726. **Thesea,** acc. sg.

l. 726. **quem,** object of **adloquitur.**

l. 727. **deum,** gen. pl.

l. 728. **talibus,** sc. **verbis.**

l. 728. **sunt,** ' (some) there are ' ; similarly in l. 730.

l. 729. **renovamine,** ' new state '.

l. 730. **quibus ius est,** ' to whom there is the power ', i.e. ' who have the power '.

l. 730. **plures,** ' many '.

l. 730. **transire,** ' to transform themselves '.

l. 731. **ut tibi,** ' as (there is) to thee ', i.e. ' as thou hast '.

l. 731. **complexi,** gen. sg. neut. Perfect participles of deponent verbs are often used with a present meaning. Translate by a relative clause.

l. 731. **Proteu,** voc. sg., with **incola** in apposition.

l. 732. **iuvenem,** ' (as) a young man '. Similarly **leonem,** and **lapis** and **arbor,** l. 735.

l. 732. **videre,** 3rd pl. perf. as scansion shows : ' (men) saw '.

l. 733. **quem tetigisse timerent. quem** refers to **anguis,** l. 734.

l. 733. **tetigisse.** No perfect meaning here. For metrical reasons, and perhaps because Greek has an aorist infinitive of which the meaning is often present, the Latin poets frequently use the perf. inf. as an alternative to the present.

l. 733. **timerent,** probably potential subjunctive, ' would fear '.

l. 735. **videri,** ' appear '.

l. 738. **minus iuris,** ' less of power ' = ' less power '. iuris is partitive genitive.

l. 738. **Erysichthone,** abl. of origin. Cf. **Ixione natus,** l. 613.

l. 739. **erat, qui,** ' was (one) who '.

l. 739. **sperneret, adoleret,** generic subjunctives. This subjunctive, a kind of consecutive, is used in relative clauses where the antecedent is general and indefinite. Cf. **non is sum qui talia credam,** ' I am not *the-sort-of-man* to believe such things '.

l. 740. **aris,** local abl., ' on the altars '.

l. 740. **nullos adoleret odores,** ' burned no fragrant offerings '.

l. 743. **annoso robore,** abl. of description, or quality. ' Having the strength of years '.

l. 744. **una nemus,** ' a forest alone ', i.e. ' a forest in itself '.

l. 744. **vittae.** These ' fillets ' were bands or chaplets, tied about the altar.

l. 744. **mediam** agrees with **eam** (= **quercum**) understood : ' its middle '.

l. 744. **memores,** ' votive '. Such tablets of acknowledgment of divine favour are still to be seen in Roman Catholic churches, especially abroad.

l. 745. **voti potentis,** ' of powerful (i.e. granted) prayer '.

l. 747. **ex ordine,** ' in order '.

l. 749. **nec non.** The two negatives cancel out, and the expression is then a useful equivalent, of two long syllables, for **et.** Here, with the following **et,** the translation is ' and indeed '.

ll. 749, 750. **cetera . . . omni,** the rest of the wood was as much lower than (**sub**) this (oak) as the grass was lower than all the wood '. tanto, quanto, ablatives of the measure of difference.

l. 751. Triopeïus = Erysichthon.

l. 751. illā, i.e. from the oak.

l. 752. -que, ' but '.

l. 753. ut, ' when '.

l. 753. iussos, ' (though so) bidden '. The participle agrees with eos understood, and does the work of a concessive clause.

l. 754. The order is securi rapta ab uno sceleratus edidit haec verba.

ll. 755, 756. non dilecta . . . sit dea, ' not only (though) beloved by the goddess, but even though (licebit) it be the goddess herself '.

l. 755. deae, dative of the agent.

l. 755. licebit. The future has the same meaning here as the present licet when it is virtually a conjunction (= ' although '), taking the subjunctive.

l. 756. tanget. The subject is, of course, the holy oak.

l. 757. obliquos in ictus, ' for a slanting blow ', pl. for sg.

l. 760. ducere, ' to assume '.

l. 762. haud aliter quam, ' not otherwise than ', i.e. ' just as '.

l. 763. solet. The subject is cruor, l. 764.

l. 763. victima, in apposition to taurus.

l. 765. ex omnibus, ' among them all '.

l. 769. repetitaque robora caedit, ' and hews at the tree, attacked anew ', i.e. ' and attacking the tree anew, hews at it '.

l. 772. tibi, dat. of disadvantage, with instare.

l. 772. poenas instare, acc. + infin. dependent on vaticinor, l. 773. ' I prophesy that punishment is at hand '.

l. 773. nostri, pl. for sg.

l. 773. **solacia,** in apposition to the indirect statement, **poenas instare.**

l. 776. **multam silvam,** ' much of the wood '.

l. 777. **Dryades,** with **omnes germanae.**

l. 777. **damno nemorumque suoque,** ' both by their own and the forest's loss '.

l. 778. **cum,** prep.

l. 780. **his,** the Dryads.

l. 780. **pulcherrima,** between commas in English, ' (goddess) most fair '.

l. 782. **si non ... actis,** ' except that, by reason of his deeds, he was not to be pitied by anyone '.

l. 783. **nulli,** dat. of the agent, usual after adjectives in **-bilis.**

l. 784. **lacerare,** in apposition to **genus,** l. 782, ' (namely) to rack him '.

l. 784. **ipsi deae,** dat. of the agent with the gerundive **adeunda :** ' since she (**quae** = **Fames**) is not to be approached by the goddess in person (**ipsi**) '.

l. 786. **montani numinis,** collective. Translate by plural.

l. 791. **ea se ... condat ... iube,** ' command that she hide herself '. **condat** depends on **ut** understood. The expression is unusual, as **iubeo** normally takes the infinitive.

l. 792. **rerum,** ' of food-stuffs '.

l. 793. **superetque.** **Fames** is the subject, a rather abrupt change.

l. 794. **neve** = **et ne,** ' and that ... not '.

l. 794. **currus,** pl. for sg., ' (my) chariot '.

l. 795. **moderere.** Final subjunctive, ' to drive '.

l. 795. **dracones,** plainly ' (winged) serpents ', as **alte** shows.

l. 796. **dedit.** The object is **eos** (= **currus et dracones**) understood.

l. 796. **subvecta,** nom. sg. fem., ' up-borne ', i.e. ' soaring '.

l. 797. **rigidi,** ' frozen '.

l. 797. **cacumine,** local abl. without prep., ' on the top '.

l. 798. **Caucason,** acc. sg., agreeing with **eum (=montem)** understood.

l. 798. **serpentum colla levavit,** i.e. she unyoked them.

l. 799. **quaesitam,** ' after a search ', lit. ' having been sought '.

l. 802. **situ, rubigine,** abls. of cause.

l. 803. **dura,** ' stretched tight '.

l. 803. **per quam,** etc., ' so that through it there could be seen '.

l. 803. **possent,** consecutive subjunctive.

l. 805. **ventris** depends on **locus.**

l. 805. **putares,** a potential subjunctive, which is really a conditional with the if-clause understood : ' you would have thought ' (if you had been there to see).

l. 805. **pendere,** ' hung (free) ', i.e. unsupported by the body below.

l. 806. **a crate.** The use of a preposition with the abl. of the instrument is unusual. Cf. l. 379.

l. 806. **crate spinae,** ' the framework of the spine '. The ribs are meant.

l. 807. **auxerat.** Not by increasing the size, but by making them seem larger relatively to the wasted flesh.

l. 808. **prodibant,** ' stuck out ', ' bulged '.

l. 808. **immodico tubere,** abl. of manner, ' in great swellings '.

l. 809. **neque enim,** etc., explains **procul.**

l. 812. **visa,** sc. **est.**

l. 812. **sensisse.** See note on **tetigisse,** l. 733.

l. 813. **versis habenis,** not really ' turning the reins ', but rather ' turning them (i.e. the dracones) *with* the reins '.

l. 814. **quamvis** with the indicative is frequent in Ovid. In prose it normally takes the subjunctive.

l. 816. **iussam,** ' appointed '.

l. 816. **delata est,** ' was carried '.

l. 817. **solutum,** ' relaxed ', agrees with **eum** (= Erysichthona) understood.

l. 818. **ulnis,** ' arms ', lit. ' elbows ', a use of the part for the whole.

l. 819. **viro,** dative of disadvantage with **inspirat.**

l. 820. **vacuis,** ' hollow ' ; **spargit,** ' sowed '.

l. 821. **mandato,** governed by **functa.**

l. 824. **sub imagine somni,** i.e. he dreams of feasting.

l. 825. **ora,** ' jaws '.

l. 828. **ardor,** ' craving '.

l. 829. **immensa,** ' cavernous '.

l. 830. **quod pontus . . . educat aër.** Take all this after **poscit,** and supply **id** (object of **poscit**) as antecedent. **(id) quod** then = ' all, that '.

l. 831. **appositis mensis.** The abl. abs. is equivalent to a concessive (' although ') clause.

l. 832. **in,** ' in the midst of '.

l. 832. **quod.** Supply as antecedent **id,** subject to **poterat esse satis,** ' what could satisfy '.

l. 832. **urbibus,** ' (whole) cities '.

l. 834. **plusque.** Supply **eo,** and take the whole **quo** clause first. ' The more he lowers . . . the more he desires '. **eo** and **quo** are ablatives of the measure of difference, lit. ' by which (amount) he lowers more . . . by that (amount) he desires more '.

l. 836. **-que,** ' but ', and similarly the **-que** in l. 838.

l. 839. **plura.** Supply **eo** and see the note on l. 834.

l. 839. **turba,** abl. of cause, ' because of the quantity (supplied) '.

l. 840. **ora,** ' lips ', as often in the plural.

l. 842. **cibi,** ' of (desiring) food '.

l. 842. **locus,** i.e. his belly.

l. 844. **attenuarat,** syncopated form of the pluperfect.

l. 845. **vigebat,** ' burned '.

l. 847. **non . . . parente,** ' not worthy of that father ', i.e. ' worthy of a better father '.   Note the usual ablative after **dignus.**

l. 848. **inops,** ' in his poverty '.

l. 849. **generosa,** ' the noble (girl) '.

l. 850. She prays to her lover, Neptune.

l. 850. **o qui,** ' O thou who '.

l. 850. **nobis,** ' from me ' (pl. for sg.) ;   dat. of disadvantage going with **raptae.**

l. 851. **haec** = **praemia.**

l. 852. **quamvis . . . ero,** ' though she had just been seen by her master, who was following her '.   **quamvis** here takes the subjunctive.   **ero,** dat. of the agent.   **sequenti,** observe the participle doing the work of a relative clause.

l. 853. The first **-que** (lit. ' both ') need not be translated.

l. 854. **et cultus . . . aptos,** ' and a dress suited to (men) taking fish ', i.e. ' and clothes proper to a fisherman '.

l. 856. **aera,** ' hook ' (of bronze).

l. 857. **mare** subject to **sit** (optative subjunctive, expressing a wish) understood :   ' so may the sea be calm '.   It is very common in Latin to preface a request with such a wish for the well-being of the person addressed.   In such a case the wish is usually introduced by **sic** or **ita,** serving to indicate that the good wishes are conditional upon the fulfilment of the following request.

l. 858. **nisi fixus,** ' unless pierced ', i.e. ' until you have struck him '.

ll. 859, 860. Take **dic ubi sit** from l. 861 before these two lines :   ' say where she is, who . . . '

l. 859. **turbatis capillis,** abl. of description or quality.

l. 860. **steterat.** English idiom requires imperfect or aorist here.

l. 860. **stantem** agrees with **eam** (object of **vidi**) understood.

l. 861. **exstant,** ' are visible ', i.e. her tracks come to an end.

l. 862. **bene cedere,** ' was turning out well '.

l. 862. **a se se quaeri gaudens,** ' rejoicing that she was being enquired for from herself ', i.e. ' that she was being questioned about herself '—rejoicing, of course, because such questioning made it plain that her disguise was completely effective.

l. 863. **his** sc. **verbis.**

l. 863. **est resecuta rogantem,** ' answered (him) enquiring ', i.e. ' answered his enquiry '.

l. 864. **ignoscas,** 2nd pers. jussive subjunctive, equivalent to an imperative.

l. 864. **lumina,** ' eyes ', as often.

l. 864. **partem,** ' direction '.

l. 865. **studio operatus inhaesi. operatus** and **inhaesi** both govern **studio** (dat.) : ' I have stuck to my pursuit, absorbed in it '.

l. 866. **quoque minus dubites.** See note on l. 579 and cf. l. 620.

l. 866. **sic.** See note on **mare,** l. 857. In the present case, however, the conditional good wishes benefit the speaker and are meant to guarantee the truth of a following statement, which is introduced by **ut** (l. 867)—best left untranslated—balancing **sic.** Cf. English, ' I didn't do it, *so help me God*'.

l. 866. **has artes,** i.e. her fishing (pl. for sg.).

l. 867. **nemo,** ' no man '.

l. 871. The order is: **Ast ubi pater sensit suam (filiam) habere corpora transformia. transformia,** ' capable of changing its form '.

I

l. 872. **Triopeïda,** five syllables. ' The child of Triopas ' is really his grand-daughter, and daughter of Erysichthon.

l. 873. **nunc equa,** ' now (as) a mare,' etc.

l. 874. **non iusta,** ' stolen '.

l. 875. **postquam,** as usual, best translated ' when '.
Apparently the trick of continually selling his daughter became too widely known, or else she ceased to be available for these duties on her marriage to Autolycus—another famous trickster—alluded to in l. 738.

l. 877. **lacero,** ' tearing '.

l. 878. **infelix,** nom. sg. masc., ' unhappy wretch '.

l. 878. **minuendo corpus alebat,** ' nourished his body by consuming it '. An example of oxymoron. See note on l. 477.

l. 879. **quid moror externis?** ' Why do I dwell on outside instances? ' As Achelous goes on to say, he himself has the power of assuming other forms.

l. 879. **novandi,** gerundive, not gerund, as its agreement with **corporis** shows.

l. 879. **mihi est,** ' there is to me ', i.e. ' I have '. Dative of the possessor.

l. 880. **iuvenis,** i.e. Theseus. Cf. l. 726.

l. 881. **(is) qui,** ' what ' or ' as '.

l. 882. **dux,** ' (as) leader '. i.e. he takes the form of a bull. River gods were commonly represented in art under this guise.

l. 883. **pars,** ' side '. **telo,** abl., governed by **caret.** The lost horn was broken off in a struggle with Heracles.

VOCABULARY

In the following vocabulary only irregular verbs are given their principal parts in full. Otherwise the figures (1), (2), (3), (4) *following a verb denote that it is a regular example of that conjugation. No conjugation number is given in the case of* -io *verbs like* capio.

The long vowels least likely to be known have been marked long.

ā, *interj.*, ah!

ā, ab, *prep. with abl.*, from, by ; after.

abdo, -ere, -didi, -ditum (3), hide.

abeo, -īre, -ii, -itum, go away, pass.

abrumpo, -ere, -rūpi, -ruptum (3), break off, sever.

abscīdo, -ere, -cīdi, -cīsum (3), cut off.

absēns, -sentis, absent.

abstineo, -ēre, -tinui, -tentum (2), keep off, refrain.

absum, -esse, āfui, be away, be far off.

ac, and ; *after* secus, than.

Acarnānes, -um, *m. pl.*, Acarnanians, people of Acarnania.

Acastus, -i, *m.*, Acastus, son of Pelias ; one of the boar-hunters.

accēdo, -ere, -cessi, -cessum (3), come to, be added (to).

accipio, -ere, -cēpi, -ceptum, receive, accept.

accommodo (1), fit.

accumbo, -ere, -cubui, -cubitum (3), lie down.

ācer, ācris, ācre, sharp, fierce, eager.

acernus, -a, -um, of maple.

acerra, -ae, *f.*, censer, incense box.

Achāīa (Achāïa, l. 268), -ae, *f.*, Achaea, Greece.

Achelōus, -i, *m.*, Achelous, a river of Western Greece, flowing between Acarnania and Aetolia ; the god of the river.

Achilles, -is, *m.*, Achilles, son of Peleus.

Actaeus, -a, -um, Athenian.

Actorides, -ae, *m.*, son of Actor (Eurytus *or* Cleatus).

actum, -i, *n.*, deed.

acūmen, -inis, *n.*, point.

acūtus, -a, -um, sharp.

ad, *prep. with acc.*, to, towards; for; as regards.

addo, -ere, -didi, -ditum (3), add, give, join, bring.

addūco, -ere, -dūxi, -dūctum (3), bring to, pull to, pull tight.

adeo, -īre, -ii, -itum, go to, approach.

adfectus, -ūs, *m.*, passion, emotion.

adfero, -ferre, attuli, allatum, bring to.

adflātus, -ūs, *m.*, breath.

adflo (1), breathe upon.

adfor, -fari, -fatus sum (1 *dep.*), address.

adfundo, -ere, -fūdi, -fūsum (3), pour on, cast on.

adhūc, as yet, still.

adimo, -ere, -ēmi, -emptum (3), take away.

adipīscor, -i, adeptus sum (3 *dep.*), obtain.

aditus, -ūs, *m.*, entrance.

adiuvo, -are, -iūvi, -iūtum (1), help.

adlevo (1), lift up.

adloquor, -i, -locutus sum (3 *dep.*), address.

admoveo, -ēre, -mōvi, -mōtum (2), bring to, put to *or* near (+*dat.*).

adnuo, -ere, -nui, -nutum (3), nod in assent, assent.

adoleo, -ēre, -ui, -ultum (2), offer, burn.

adoperio, -īre, -erui, -ertum (4), cover over.

adoro (1), worship.

adpōno, -ere, -posui, -positum (3), put to, add, place beside.

adsuesco, -ere, -suēvi, -suētum (3), be accustomed.

adsum, -esse, -fui, be present, be here, come.

aduncus, -a, -um, hooked, bent, curved.

adūro, -ere, -ussi, -ustum (3), burn (*transitive*).

adversus, -a, -um, facing.

adverto, -ere, -verti, -versum (3), turn to (*transitive*).

Aeacides, -ae, *m.*, son of Aeacus, Peleus *or* Telamon.

Aegīdes, -ae, *m.*, son of Aegeus, Theseus.

aegrē fero, take ill, resent.

ăēnum, -i, *n.,* brazen vessel, cauldron.

aequālis, -e, equal.

aequo (1), make equal, level ; *in pass.,* be equal (l. 288).

aequor, -is, *n.,* sea.

aequus, -a, -um, equal, level.

āēr, -is, *m.,* air.

aerātus, -a, -um, of bronze, bronze-plated.

aes, aeris, *n.,* bronze, object made of bronze ; fish-hook.

aesculeus, -a, -um, oak, of oak.

Aesonides, -ae, *m.,* son of Aeson, Jason.

aestus, -ūs, *m.,* boiling, heat ; tide.

aetas, -ātis, *f.,* age.

aether, -is, *m.,* sky, heaven.

Aetnaeus, -a, -um, of Etna, Sicilian.

aevum, -i, *n.,* age.

ager, -gri, *m.,* land, field.

agito (1), drive, disturb.

āgmen, -inis, *n.,* line, band, company.

ago, -ere, ēgi, actum (3), do, drive ; spend *or* pass time ; iter **agere,** direct one's course ; **nihil agere,** achieve nothing.

agrestis, -e, of the country, rustic, wild.

agricola, -ae, *m.,* farmer.

aio (ait, aiunt), *defective verb,* say.

āla, -ae, *f.,* wing.

albus, -a, -um, white.

Alcathous, -i, *m.,* Alcathous, son of Pelops.

Alcmēna, -ae, *f.,* Alcmena, wife of Amphitryon and mother of Hercules.

āles, -itis, *c.,* bird.

aliēnus, -a, -um, belonging to another.

alimentum, -i, *n.,* nourishment, fuel.

aliquis, -qua, -quid, some-one, something.

aliter, otherwise.

alius, -a, -ud, other.

alligo (1), bind.

alo, -ere, alui, altum (3), feed, nourish.

altē, on high.

alter, -a, -um, one, *or* the other (*of two*).

alternus, -a, -um, alternate.

Althaea, -ae, *f.,* Althaea, daughter of Thestius, wife of Oeneus, mother of Meleager.

altus, -a, -um, high, deep.

alveus, -i, *m.,* hollow, (*river*) bed.

alvus, -i, *f.,* belly.

ambāges, -is, *f.,* winding.

ambiguus, -a, -um, doubtful.

ambitiōsus, -a, -um, seeking much ; much sought (l. 277).

ambo, -ae, -o, both.

amnis, -is, *m.,* river.

amo (1), love.

amor, -ōris, *m.,* love.

amplector, -i, -plexus sum (3 *dep.*), clasp, embrace.

amplexus, -ūs, *m.,* embrace, love.

Ampycides, -ae, *m.,* son of Ampyx, Mopsus.

Amyclae, -arum, *f. pl.,* Amyclae, town of Laconia in Greece.

Amyntor, -oris, *m.,* Amyntor, King of the Dolopes, and father of Phoenix.

an, or.

Ancaeus, -i, *m.,* Ancaeus.

anceps, -ipitis, two-headed, two-edged.

anguis, -is, *m.,* snake.

anīlis, -e, of an old woman, aged.

anima, -ae, *f.,* breath, life ; spirit, ghost.

animus, -i, *m.,* mind ; *in pl.,* courage, spirit, wrath.

annōsus, -a, -um, aged, full of years.

annus, -i, *m.,* year.

ānser, -eris, *m.,* goose, gander.

ante, *prep. with acc.,* before, beyond ; *as adv.,* before, in front.

antīquus, -a, -um, ancient, former.

antrum, -i, *n.,* cave.

anus, -ūs, *f.,* old woman.

aper, -pri, *m.,* (*wild*) boar.

aperio, -īre, -erui, -ertum (4), open, reveal.

Apharēïus, -a, -um, of Aphareus, King of Messene.

appello (1), call.

appōno, -ere, -posui, -positum (3), set near, place before.

aptus, -a, -um, suitable, fit.

aqua, -ae, *f.*, water.

āra, -ae, *f.*, altar.

arātor, -ōris, *m.*, ploughman.

arbor, -is, *f.*, tree.

arboreus, -a, -um, of a tree.

Arcas, -adis, *m.*, Arcadian ; =Ancaeus in l. 391.

arcus, -ūs, *m.*, bow.

ardeo, -ēre, arsi, arsum, burn (*intransitive*) ; blaze, be on fire, be in love.

ardor, -ōris, *m.*, heat, passion, craving.

arduus, -a, -um, high, steep.

ārea, -ae, *f.*, threshing-floor.

argentum, -i, *n.*, silver-plate.

Argolicus, -a, -um, Greek.

argūmentum, -i, *n.*, proof, token.

āridus, -a, -um, dry.

arma, -orum, *n. pl.*, arms, weapons.

Armenius, -a, -um, of Armenia.

armentum, -i, *n.*, head of cattle, ox ; herd.

armus, -i, *m.*, shoulder.

ars, -tis, *f.*, art, skill, cunning, accomplishment.

articulus, -i, *m.*, joint.

artus, -ūs, *m.*, limb.

arvum, -i, *n.*, field, land.

arx, arcis, *f.*, citadel, tower.

ascendo, -ere, -di, -sum (3), climb, mount.

aspicio, -ere, -spēxi, -spectum, behold, look at.

ast, but.

asto, -are, -stiti (1), stand by, stand near.

at, but, yet.

āter, -tra, -trum, black.

Athēnae, -arum, *f. pl.*, Athens.

Atlantiades, -ae, *m.*, son of Atlas, Mercury.

atque, and, and moreover.
atrium, -i, *n.*, hall.
attenuo (1), diminish.
attonitus, -a, -um, astonished, appalled.
auctor, -ōris, *m.*, originator, author ; thrower, l. 349.
audācia, -ae, *f.*, daring.
audāx, -ācis, daring.
audeo, -ēre, ausus sum (2 *semi-dep.*), dare.
audio (4), hear.
aufero, -ferre, abstuli, ablatum, carry away, take from.
augeo, -ēre, auxi, auctum (2), increase (*transitive*), enlarge.
aura, -ae, *f.*, breeze, air.
aurātus, -a, -um, gilded, gilt, golden.
auris, -is, *f.*, ear.
aurum, -i, *n.*, gold.
Auster, -tri, *m.*, South wind.
aut, either, or.
Autolycus, -i, *m.*, Autolycus, son of Mercury.
autumnālis, -e, of autumn.
avēna, -ae, *f.*, oat-straw.
āverto, -ere, -ti, -sum (3), turn aside *or* away (*transitive*).
avidus, -a, -um, greedy.
avis, -is, *f.*, bird.

baca, -ae, *f.*, berry.
baculum, -i, *n.*, staff, stick.
Baucis, -idis, *f.*, Baucis.
beātus, -a, -um, blessed, happy.
bellātrix, -īcis, *f.*, (*female*) warrior ; war-like.
bellum, -i, *n.*, war.
bene, well.
bicolor, -oris, of two colours.
bicornis, -e, two-horned, two-pronged.
bipennifer, -a, -um, bearing an axe.
bipennis, -is, *f.*, axe.
bis, twice.

bonus, -a, -um, good, kind.

Böötes, -ae, *m.*, the Waggoner, name of a constellation, near Charles' Wain (the Great Bear) of which he was fancifully likened to the driver.

bōs, bovis, *c.*, bull, ox, cow.

bracchium, -i, *n.*, arm.

brevis, -e, short.

bustum, -i, *n.*, tomb.

cacūmen, -inis, *n.*, top.

cado, -ere, cecidi, cāsum (3), fall.

cādūcifer, -a, -um, bearing the caduceus, or herald's staff.

caecus, -a, -um, blind, dark ; unseen.

caedes, -is, *f.*, slaughter.

caedo, -ere, cecīdi, caesum (3), cut.

caelestis, -e, of heaven.

caelicola, -ae, *c.*, dweller in heaven, god.

caelo (1), carve, engrave.

caelum, -i, *n.*, heaven.

Caenēus, -ei, *m.*, Caeneus, one of the boar-hunters.

caeruleus, -a, -um, blue.

caestus, -ūs, *m.*, boxing-glove.

calamus, -i, *m.*, reed, arrow.

caleo (2), be warm, be hot.

calidus, -a, -um, warm.

Calydon, -ōnis, *f.*, town in Aetolia.

Calydōnis, -idis, *f.*, woman of Calydon.

Calydōnius, -a, -um, Calydonian.

Calymnē, -ēs, *f.*, Calymne, one of the Sporades (' scattered islands ') in the Aegean.

candidus, -a, -um, white, gleaming.

cānì, -orum, *m. pl.*, grey hairs.

canis, -is, *c.*, dog, hound.

canistrum, -i, *n.*, basket.

cānities, -ei, *f.*, grey hairs.

canna, -ae, *f.*, reed, cane.

cantus, -ūs, *m.*, music, song, note.

cānus, -a, -um, white, grey, hoary.

capax, -ācis, capacious, capable of.

capillus, -i, *m.*, hair.

capio, -ere, cēpi, captum, take, catch, conquer, hold, contain.

capto (1), strive to catch, angle for (l. 217).

caput, -itis, *n.*, head.

careo (2), lack, want (+ *abl.*).

cārica, -ae, *f.*, dried fig.

carīna, -ae, *f.*, ship (*properly*, keel).

carmen, -inis, *n.*, song ; incantation.

carpo, -ere, -psi, -ptum (3), pluck ; traverse, l. 210.

cārus, -a, -um, dear.

casa, -ae, *f.*, cottage, hut.

cassis, -idis, *f.*, helmet.

castra, -orum, *n. pl.*, camp.

cāsus, -ūs, *m.*, chance, fate, fortune.

Caucasus, -i, *m.*, Caucasus.

causa, -ae, *f.*, cause, case, reason.

cavus, -a, -um, hollow.

Cecropides, -ae, *m.*, son of Cecrops, Theseus.

cēdo, -ere, cessi, cessum (3), yield, retire, result.

celeber, -bris, -bre, frequented, thronged, famous, rich (*in*).

celer, -ris, -re, swift.

cēlo (1), hide, conceal.

celsus, -a, -um, high, lofty.

cēnsus, -ūs, *m.*, income, estate.

centum, a hundred.

Cephalus, -i, *m.*, Cephalus.

cēra, -ae, *f.*, wax.

Cereālis, -e, of Ceres.

Ceres, -eris, *f.*, Ceres, goddess of agriculture ; *used for* corn, grain (l. 292).

cerno, -ere, crēvi, crētum (3), see.

certāmen, -inis, *n.*, contest.

certē, certainly, at least.

certus, -a, -um, sure, certain, fixed.

cervix, -īcis, *f.*, neck.

cervus, -i, *m.*, stag.

cesso (1), be idle, stand idle.

cēterus, -a, -um, remaining, the rest.

Charybdis, -is, *f.*, Charybdis, famous whirlpool in the Straits of Messina.

chorea, -ae, *f.*, dance.

cibus, -i, *m.*, food.

cingo, -ere, cinxi, cinctum (3), surround, encircle.

cinis, -eris, *m.*, ash, ashes.

circueo (circumeo), -ire, -ii, -itum, go round.

circumdo, -dare, -dedi, -datum (1), surround.

cīris, -is, *f.*, Ciris, name of the bird into which Scylla was changed.

citrā, *prep. with acc.*, on this side of, before.

cīvis, -is, *c.*, citizen.

clādes, -is, *f.*, disaster.

clāmo (1), shout, cry out.

clāmor, -ōris, *m.*, shout, cry.

clārus, -a, -um, bright, famous.

classis, -is, *f.*, fleet.

claudo, -ere, -si, -sum (3), shut, close, shut in.

claustrum, -i, *n.*, bar, lock, bolt, key.

clēmentia, -ae, *f.*, mercy, pity, clemency.

clipeus, -i, *m.*, shield.

clīvus, -i, *m.*, slope.

coacervo (1), heap together.

coāctus, *see* cogo.

Cōcalus, -i, *m.*, Cocalus, King of Camicus in Sicily.

coeo, -ire, -ii, -itum, come together, meet.

coepi, -isse, -tum, *defective verb*, began.

coeptum, -i, *n.*, beginning, undertaking, design, plan, purpose.

cōgnōsco, -ere, -ōvi, -itum (3), get to know, learn ; *in perf. tenses*, know.

cōgo, -ere, -ēgi, -āctum (3), drive together, curdle.

colligo, -ere, -lēgi, -lēctum (3), gather.

collis, -is, *m.*, hill.

collum, -i, *n.*, neck.

colo, -ere, colui, cultum (3), cultivate, till ; worship.
colōnus, -i, *m.*, farmer, peasant.
columna, -ae, *f.*, column, pillar.
comes, -itis, *c.*, companion.
comito (1), accompany.
committo, -ere, -mīsi, -missum (3), entrust.
commūnis, -e, common, joint.
compello (1), address.
complector, -i, -plexus sum (3 *dep.*), embrace, encircle.
compōno, -ere, -posui, -positum (3), put together.
compos, -potis, master of, in control of.
compositus, -a, -um, calm, composed.
cōnāmen, -inis, *n.*, effort, attempt.
concavus, -a, -um, hollow, deep.
concēdo, -ere, -cessi, -cessum (3), give way, yield.
concha, -ae, *f.*, shell.
concido, -ere, -cidi (3), fall.
concio (4), urge, rouse, speed.
concipio, -ere, -cēpi, -ceptum, take hold of ; draw up,
    repeat, l. 682.
concordia, -ae, *f.*, harmony ; partnership.
concors, -dis, harmonious.
concutio, -ere, -cussi, -cussum, shake.
condo, -ere, -didi, -ditum (3), store up, bury ; pickle, l. 665.
cōnfugio, -ere, -fūgi, flee for refuge.
congero, -ere, -gessi, -gestum (3), heap up, pile up.
cōnicio, -ere, -iēci, -iectum, hurl.
coniungo, -ere, -iunxi, -iunctum (3), join.
coniunx, -iugis, *c.*, spouse ; husband, wife.
cōnor (1 *dep.*), try.
cōnsanguineus, -a, -um, related by blood.
cōnscius, -a, -um, conscious ; *as noun*, accomplice.
cōnsenesco, -ere, -senui (3), grow old together.
cōnsequor, -i, -secūtus sum (3 *dep.*), follow up, reach, attain.
cōnsilium, -i, *n.*, advice, counsel, plan.
cōnsisto, -ere, -stiti (3), come to a halt, stand (still).
cōnsors, -tis, having the same lot *or* portion ; of a brother *or*
    sister ; *as noun*, co-heir ; brother.

cōnspicio, -ere, -spexi, -spectum, catch sight of, see, behold.

cōnspicuus, -a, -um, bright, clear, conspicuous.

cōnsuesco, -ere, -suēvi, -suētum (3), grow accustomed ; *in perf. tenses*, be accustomed.

cōnsumo, -ere, -sumpsi, -sumptum (3), devour, exhaust, use up.

conterminus, -a, -um, adjacent, neighbouring.

contingo, -ere, -tigi, -tactum (3), touch, reach.

continuus, -a, -um, continuous ; unbroken, l. 588.

contorqueo, -ēre, -torsi, -tortum (2), hurl.

contrā, *prep. with acc.*, against.

contrārius, -a, -um, opposed, contrary.

contremesco, -ere, -tremui (3), tremble greatly.

convalesco, -ere, -valui (3), gain strength, grow strong.

converto, -ere, -verti, -versum (3), turn (*transitive*).

cōpia, -ae, *f.*, plenty, abundance ; quantity.

corneus, -a, -um, horny.

cornū, -ūs, *n.*, horn ; wing (*of an army*).

cornum, -i, *n.*, cornel-tree, cornel wood ; spear of cornel-wood ; cornel-cherry, l. 665.

corōna, -ae, *f.*, crown, diadem.

corōno (1), crown, wreathe, deck.

corpus, -oris, *n.*, body.

corripio, -ere, -ripui, -reptum, catch, seize.

corruo, -ere, -rui (3), fall, collapse.

cortex, -icis, *m.*, bark (*of tree*).

crātēr, -is, *m.*, mixing-bowl.

crātis, -is, *f.*, wicker-work, basket ; wicker-like frame.

creātor, -ōris, *m.*, father.

crēdo, -ere, -didi, -ditum (3), believe (+*dat. of person believed*).

crēdulus, -a, -um, credulous, confiding.

cremo (1), burn.

crēsco, -ere, crēvi, crētum, grow (*intransitive*).

Crētē, -es, *f.*, Crete.

crētus, -a, -um (*from* crēsco), sprung (from).

crīmen, -inis, *n.*, charge ; crime.

crīnis, -is, *m.*, hair, lock, tress.

cristātus, -a, -um, plumed, crested.
crūdēlis, -e, cruel.
cruento (1), stain with blood, make bloody.
cruor, -ōris, *m.*, blood.
cubīle, -is, *m.*, bed; *in pl.*, l. 55, marriage.
cubitum, -i, *n.*, elbow.
cultus, -ūs, *m.*, refinement; dress.
cum, *prep. with abl.*, with, together with.
cum, *conj.*, when, since, although.
cunctor (1 *dep.*), delay.
cunctus, -a, -um, all.
cupīdo, -inis, *f.* (*m.* in l. 74), desire, love.
cupio, -ere, -īvi, -ītum, desire.
cūr, why.
cūra, -ae, *f.*, care, trouble, concern; object of care (l. 724).
Cūrētis, -idos, Cretan; *lit.* of the Curetes.
curro, -ere, cucurri, cursum (3), run, speed.
currus, -ūs, *m.*, chariot.
cursus, -ūs, *m.*, course, voyage; running, l. 311.
curvāmen, -inis, *n.*, curve.
cuspis, -idis, *f.*, spear, spear-point.
custōdia, -ae, *f.*, guard.
custos, -ōdis, *c.*, guard, keeper.
cutis, -is, *m.*, skin.
Cydoneus, -a, -um, Cydonian, Cretan.

Daedalus, -i, *m.*, Daedalus, famous craftsman of mythology.
damnōsus, -a, -um, harmful, ruinous.
damnum, -i, *n.*, harm, loss.
(daps), dapis, *f.*, feast, banquet.
dē, *prep. with abl.*, from, down from; out of, of; about, concerning.
dea, -ae, *f.*, goddess.
deceo (2), become, befit.
dēcipio, -ere, -cēpi, -ceptum, deceive.

decoro (1), adorn.

decus, -oris, *n.*, grace, glory, beauty (l. 536).

dēdūco, -ere, -dūxi, -dūctum (3), draw down, launch.

dēfendo, -ere, -di, -sum (3), defend.

dēfero, -ferre, -tuli, -lātum, bring down, float down.

dēficio, -ere, -fēci, -fectum, fail, lose strength.

dēfleo, -ēre, -flēvi, -flētum (2), weep for, bewail.

Dēlos, -i, *f.*, Delos, Aegean island, birth-place of Apollo and Diana.

dēlūbrum, -i, *n.*, shrine, temple.

dēlūdo, -ere, -si, -sum (3), mock, deceive.

dēmissus, -a, -um, low.

dēmitto, -ere, -mīsi, -missum (3), send down, pour down.

dēmo, -ere, -psi, -ptum (3), take away.

dēnique, at length.

dēns, dentis, *m.*, tooth, tusk.

Dēōius, -a, -um, sacred to Ceres.

dēpōno, -ere, -posui, -positum (3), put down, lay aside.

dērigo, -ere, -rexi, -rectum (3), guide, direct, aim.

dēsero, -ere, -serui, -sertum (3), desert, forsake.

dēsino, -ere, -sii, -situm (3), cease.

despicio, -ere, -spexi, -spectum, look down on.

destino (1), resolve.

destituo, -ere, -ui, -utum (3), abandon.

destringo, -ere, -nxi, -ctum (3), strip off, graze.

dēterreo (2), frighten from, prevent.

dētrunco (1), lop off, cut off.

deus, -i, *m.*, god.

dēvenio, -ire, -vēni, -ventum (4), arrive.

dēvexus, -a, -um, sloping down.

dēvoro (1), devour, swallow down.

dēvoveo, -ēre, -vōvi, -vōtum (2), vow to the (infernal) gods, curse.

dexter, -t(e)ra, -t(e)rum, right, right hand, on the right.

dextra, -ae, *f.*, right-hand.

dī, *nom. pl. of* deus.

Dia, -ae, *f.*, Dia, another name for Naxos, Aegean island on which Ariadne was abandoned.

Diāna, -ae, *f.,* Diana, daughter of Jupiter by Latona ; goddess of the chase.

dīco, -ere, -xi, -ctum (3), say, name, call.

Dictaeus, -a, -um, of Dicte, Cretan mountain on which Jupiter was hidden from his father as a babe ; *hence* Cretan.

dīctum, -i, *n.,* word.

dīdūco, -ere, -dūxi, -dūctum (3), part, separate.

dies, -ēī, *m.* (*rarely* f.), day.

difficilis, -e, difficult.

diffugio, -ere, -fūgi, flee in different directions, scatter in flight.

digitus, -i, *m.,* finger, toe.

dīgnor (1 *dep.*), deem worthy.

dīgnus, -a, -um, worthy.

dīligo, -ere, -lexi, -lectum (3), love.

dīmitto, -ere, -mīsi, -missum (3), send away, let go.

dīmoveo, -ēre, -mōvi, -mōtum (2), separate, part ; rake aside, l. 641.

dīrigo, -ere, -rexi, -rectum (3), aim.

dīrus, -a, -um, dread, dire.

disco, -ere, didici (3), learn.

discrīmen, -inis, *n.,* distinction, intervening space; l. 578, gap.

discumbo, -ere, -cubui, -cubitum (3), recline (*at table*).

discutio, -ere, -cussi, -cussum, shatter, split.

dispār, -is, unequal, uneven.

displiceo (2), displease (+ *dat.*).

dissipo (1), scatter.

disto, -are (1), stand apart, be different.

diu, for a long time.

diurnus, -a, -um, of the day.

dīvello, -ere, -vulsi, -vulsum (3), tear, tear apart.

dīversus, -a, -um, contrary, conflicting ; this way and that.

dīves, -itis, rich.

dīvus, -i, *m.,* god.

do, dare, dedi, datum (1), give, allow ; cause, make (l. 341), **vēla dare,** set sail.

doceo, -ēre, -ui, -tum (2), teach, tell.

doleo (2), grieve.

dolor, -ōris, *m.*, grief, pain.

dominus, -i, *m.*, master, owner.

domo (1), tame, crush ; slay ; (l. 650), cook.

domus, -ūs, *f.*, house ; household, family.

dōnec, until, while.

dōno (1), give, sacrifice.

dōnum, -i, *n.*, gift, offering.

dōs, dōtis, *f.*, dowry.

dōtālis, -e, of a dowry ; brought by dowry.

draco, -ōnis, *m.*, snake, serpent, dragon.

Dryas, -antis, *m.*, Dryas, one of the boar-hunters.

Dryas, -adis, *f.*, a Dryad (*tree nymph*).

dubito (1), doubt, hesitate.

dubius, -a, -um, doubtful, hesitating ; *neut. as noun,* doubt.

dūco, -ere, dūxi, dūctum (3), lead, draw ; (l. 760), take on ; deceive.

dum, while, until.

dummodo, provided that.

duo, -ae, -o, two.

dūrus, -a, -um, hard, cruel.

dux, ducis, *m.*, leader, guide.

ē (ex), *prep. with abl.*, out of, from.

ēbibo, -ere, -bibi, -bibitum (3), drink up.

eburneus, -a, -um, of ivory.

ecce, lo! behold!

Echīnades, -um, *f. pl.*, the Echinades, islands off the mouth of the Achelous (W. Coast of Greece).

Echīon, -onis, *m.*, Echion, son of Mercury and one of the boar-hunters.

Echīonius, -a, -um, of Echion.

ecquis, -quid, anyone, anything (*in questions*).

edo, -ere *or* ēsse, ēdi, ēsum (3), eat.

ēdo, -ere, -didi, -ditum (3), give out, make known, utter.

ēdūco, -ere, -dūxi, -dūctum (3), bring up, support.

K

efficio, -ere, -fēci, -fectum, make, render.

effugio, -ere, -fūgi, escape.

ego, mei, I.

ēgredior, -i, -gressus sum, (*dep.*) step forth, go out.

ei, alas.

ēlīdo, -ere, -līsi, -līsum (3), strike out.

Ēlis, -idis, *f.*, Elis, province of the Peloponnese.

ēlix, -icis, *m.*, ditch, channel.

ēlūdo, -ere, -lūsi, -lūsum (3), baffle, escape.

ēmico, -are, -ui (1), shoot forth.

ēminus, from *or* at a distance.

emo, -ere, ēmi, ēmptum (3), buy, obtain ; win.

Enaesimus, -i, *m.*, Enaesimus, son of Hippocoon, one of the boar-hunters.

enim, for.

ēnītor, -i, -nīxus sum, (3 *dep.*), struggle out ; bear (*children*)

ēnsis, -is, *m.*, sword.

eo, īre, ii, itum, go.

Ēpīros, -i, *f.*, Epirus, western province of Greece.

epulae, -arum, *f. pl.*, feast, banquet.

equa, -ae, *f.*, mare.

equidem, indeed.

equus, -i, *m.*, horse.

Erechthēus, -a, -um, of Erechtheus.

ergo, therefore, so.

ēripio, -ere, -ui, -reptum, snatch away, rescue.

erro (1), wander, waver.

error, -ōris, *m.*, wandering, error.

ērubesco, -ere, -bui (3), blush.

ērudio (4), train, teach.

erus, -i, *m.*, master.

Erysichthon, -onis, *m.*, Erysichthon, son of Triopas.

et, and, both, also, even.

etiam, also, even, indeed.

etiamnum, even now, still.

Eumenides, -um, *f. pl.*, the Eumenides, the Furies.

Eupalamos, -i, *m.*, Eupalamus, one of the boar-hunters.

Eurōpa, -ae *or* -es, *f.*, Europa, mother of Minos.
Eurōpaeus, -a, -um, of Europa ; *m. as noun,* son of Europa.
Eurus, -i, *m.*, Eurus, the East wind.
Eurytides, -ae, *m.*, son of Eurytus, Hippasus.
Eurytion, -ōnis, *m.*, Eurytion, one of the boar-hunters.
Evēnīnē, -es, *f.*, daughter of Evenus, i.e. woman of Calydon.
ex, *see* ē.
excēdo, -ere, -cessi, -cessum (3), go out, depart.
excido, -ere, -cidi (3), fall out, pass from.
exci(e)o, -ci(e)re, -cii, -cĭtum, call forth, rouse, start.
excipio, -ere, -cēpi, -ceptum, take out, except ; catch, l. 252.
exclāmo (1), cry out.
excutio, -ere, -cussi, -cussum, shake out, shake off ; ex-
    cussus, l. 339, clashing.
exemplum, -i, *n.*, pattern, example.
exerceo, -ēre, -ui, -itum (2), keep busy, ply, weary.
exhortor (1 *dep.*), encourage, cheer on.
exigo, -ere, -ēgī, -āctum (3), drive out, demand, enforce.
exiguus, -a, -um, small, little.
exilium, -i, *n.*, exile.
exitiābilis, -e, destructive, deadly.
exitium, -i, *n.*, destruction, ruin.
exitus, -ūs, *m.*, end.
expello, -ere, -puli, -pulsum (3), drive out, drive away, let fly.
expōno, -ere, -posui, -positum (3), put out ; banish, l. 117.
exsatio (1), satisfy, glut, sate.
exspecto (1), wait for, await, expect.
exstinctus, -a, -um, extinguished, dead.
exstinguo, -ere, -nxi, -nctum (3), put out, destroy.
exsto, -are, -stiti (1), stand out, appear, be visible.
externus, -a, -um, outside, external, foreign.
extrēmus, -a, -um, farthest, remotest.
exuviae, -arum, *f. pl.*, spoils, skin.

faber, -bra, -brum, of a carpenter.
fabrico (1), fashion, make.

fābula, -ae, f., story, tale.

facies, -ēi, f., face, countenance.

facinus, -oris, n., deed, crime.

facio, -ere, fēci, factum, do, make, cause.

factum, -i, n., deed, act.

faex, -cis, f., dregs.

fāgus, -i, f., beech.

fallācia, -ae, f., deceit, treachery.

fallo, -ere, fefelli, falsum (3), deceive, beguile (l. 651) : conceal (l. 578).

falsus, -a, -um, false.

fāma, -ae, f., rumour.

fames, -is, f., hunger ; Fames, Hunger (personified).

famulus, -i, m., slave, servant.

fātālis, -e, of fate, fateful.

fateor, -ēri, fassus sum (2 dep.), confess, own.

fatigo (1), tire, weary.

fātum, -i, n., fate, destiny, future, death.

fauces, -ium, f. pl., throat.

faveo, -ēre, fāvi, fautum, favour (+dat.).

favilla, -ae, f., ashes, embers.

favus, -i, m., honey-comb.

fax, facis, f., brand, torch.

fēcundus, -a, -um, fruitful, rich in.

fēlīciter, prosperously.

fēlix, -īcis, happy, prosperous.

fēmina, -ae, f., woman.

fēmineus, -a, -um, of a woman.

femur, -oris, n., thigh.

feritas, -tatis, f., fierceness, savagery.

fero, ferre, tuli, lātum, bear, carry, carry away ; endure ; receive ; say ; in pass., rush.

ferōx, -ōcis, warlike, spirited, fearless, headstrong.

ferreus, -a, -um, of iron.

ferrum, -i, n., iron ; sword, axe, spear-point.

ferus, -a, -um, fierce, wild ; m. as noun, wild creature, beast, brute.

ferveo, -ēre, -bui (2), boil (intransitive).

fervĭdus, -a, -um, hot.

fessus, -a, -um, tired, weary.

festus, -a, -um, festal.

fētus, -ūs, *m.*, young, produce, fruit; grape, l. 294.

fībŭla, -ae, *f.*, buckle, clasp, brooch.

fictīle, -is, *n.*, earthen-ware, earthen vessel.

fictus, -a, -um, false.

fīdes, -ĕi, *f.*, faith, fulfilment (l. 711).

fīdo, -ere, fīsus sum (2 *semi-dep.*), trust (+*dat. of person, abl. of thing*).

fīdūcia, -ae, *f.*, confidence, ground for confidence, pledge.

fīgo, -ere, fīxi, fīxum, fix, fix up ; transfix, pierce.

fĭgūra, -ae, *f.*, form, shape.

fīlia, -ae, *f.*, daughter.

fīlum, -i, *n.*, thread.

fingo, -ere, -nxi, fictum (3), fashion, mould, make up ; imagine.

fīnio (4), end, finish, bound, limit.

fīnis, -is, *m. or f.*, end, limit, bound.

fīnitĭmi, -orum, *m. pl.*, neighbours.

fīo, fīeri, factus sum, become, be made.

fistŭla, -ae, *f.*, pipe.

flagro (1), blaze.

flamma, -ae, *f.*, flame ; passion, ardour.

flāveo, -ēre (2), be yellow; *partic.*, flavens, yellow.

flāvesco, -ere (3), grow yellow.

flāvus, -a, -um, yellow, yellow-haired.

flecto, -ere, -xi, -xum (3), bend, turn, curve.

fleo, -ēre, -ēvi, -ētum (2), weep.

fluctus, -ūs, *m.*, wave.

flūmen, -inis, *n.*, river.

fluo, -ere, -xi, -xum (3), flow, run down, drop.

focus, -i, *m.*, hearth.

foedo (1), befoul, defile.

foedus, -a, -um, foul, loathsome.

folium, -i, *n.*, leaf.

fōns, -tis, *m.*, source, spring.

forent = essent.

foris, -is, *f.,* door.

forma, -ae, *f.,* shape, appearance, beauty.

formōsus, -a, -um, beautiful.

forsitan, perhaps.

forte, by chance.

fortis, -e, strong, brave.

fortūna, -ae, *f.,* fortune, issue.

Fortūna, -ae, *f.,* Fortune.

foveo, -ēre, fōvi, fōtum (2), warm, cherish.

frāgmen, -inis, *n.,* fragment, chip.

fragor, -ōris, *m.,* crash.

frango, -ere, frēgi, frāctum (3), break, crush ; weaken.

frāter, -tris, *m.,* brother.

frāternus, -a, -um, of a brother.

frendo, -ere, ——, fressum (3), gnash the teeth.

frēnum, -i, *n.,* bit, bridle, reins.

frequēns, -tis, thronging, in crowds ; thickly planted, l. 329.

fretum, -i, *n.,* strait, sea.

Frīgus, -oris, *n.,* Cold, Frost (*personified*).

frondeo, -ēre (2), be in leaf.

frondōsus, -a, -um, leafy.

frōns, -dis, *f.,* leaf.

frōns, -tis, *f.,* brow.

fruor, -i, fructus sum (3 *dep.*), enjoy (+*abl.*).

frustrā, in vain.

frutex, -icis, *m.,* shrub, growth.

frux, frūgis, *mostly in pl.,* crop, fruit, *especially* grain, corn.

fugio, -ere, fūgi, flee, escape.

fugo (1), put to flight, chase away, rout.

fulgeo, -ēre, fulsi (2), shine, gleam.

fulica, -ae, *f.,* coot (*a kind of water-fowl*).

fulmen, -inis, *n.,* thunderbolt, lightning.

fulvus, -a, -um, tawny.

fundo, -ere, fūdi, fūsum (3), pour ; lay low.

fūnereus, -a, -um, funereal, fatal.

fungor, -i, functus sum (3 *dep.*), execute, perform (+*abl.*).

fūnis, -is, *m.,* rope.

fūnus, -eris, *n.*, death.
furca, -ae, *f.*, fork ; forked prop, l. 700.
furiālis, -e, of the Furies.
furibundus, -a, -um, mad, raging, furious.
furo, -ere (3), rage.
fūtūrus, -a, -um, future, about to be.

galea, -ae, *f.*, helmet.
garrulus, -a, -um, chattering.
gaudeo, -ēre, gavīsus sum (2 *semi-dep.*), rejoice.
gaudium, -i, *n.*, joy.
gelidus, -a, -um, cold.
geminus, -a, -um, twofold, twin, double.
gemitus, -ūs, *m.*, groan, sigh.
gemma, -ae, *f.*, jewel.
gemo, -ere, -ui, -itum (3), groan.
gena, -ae, *f.*, cheek.
generōsus, -a, -um, high-born, noble.
genetrix, -īcis, *f.*, mother.
genitor, -ōris, *m.*, father.
genū, -ūs, *n.*, knee.
genus, -eris, *n.*, kind ; descent, birth, stock.
germāna, -ae, *f.*, sister.
gero, -ere, gessi, gestum (3), bear, carry on, wage.
gigno, -ere, genui, genitum (3), bear (*children*).
glaciālis, -e, icy.
gladius, -i, *m.*, sword.
glāns, -dis, *f.*, acorn.
glomero (1), mass *or* heap together.
glōria, -ae, *f.*, glory.
Gnōsiacus, -a, -um, of Gnosus, once capital of Crete ; *hence*
    Cretan.
Gnōsius, -a, -um = Gnōsiacus.
Gorgē, -es, *f.*, Gorge, sister of Meleager.
gradus, -ūs, *m.*, step.
grandaevus, -a, -um, aged.

grātus, -a, -um, pleasing.
gravidus, -a, -um, heavy, laden, teeming.
gravis, -e, heavy, severe, sore.
gravo (1), weigh down.
grex, gregis, *m.*, flock.
gula, -ae, *f.*, throat ; appetite (l. 846).
gurges, -itis, *m.*, gulf ; water, flood.
guttur, -is, *n.*, throat.

habēna, -ae, *f.*, rein.
habeo (2), have, hold, possess ; rule ; regard, consider.
habitābilis, -e, habitable.
habito (1), dwell.
habitus, -ūs, *m.*, appearance, dress.
Haemonia, -ae, *f.*, Haemonia, a name for Thessaly.
haereo, -ēre, haesi, haesum (2), stick, cling, cleave.
haliāeetos, -i, *m.*, sea-eagle, osprey.
hāmus, -i, *m.*, hook.
harēna, -ae, *f.*, sand.
harundo, -inis, *f.*, reed ; (object made of reed), arrow, fishing-rod.
hasta, -ae, *f.*, spear.
hastīle, -is, *n.*, spear.
haud, not.
haurio, -īre, hausi, haustum (4), drain, drink in, conceive ; tear open, ll. 371, 439 ; scrape up (l. 539).
Helicē, -ēs, *f.*, the Great Bear.
Helicon, -ōnis, *m.*, Helicon, mountain in Bœotia.
herba, -ae, *f.*, grass, blade (*of grass*).
herbidus, -a, -um, grassy.
hērōs, -ōis, *m.*, hero.
hesternus, -a, -um, of yesterday, yesterday's.
heu, alas!
hic, haec, hoc, this.
hīc, *adv.*, here.
hinc, hence.

Hippasus, -i, *m.,* Hippasus, son of Eurytus, one of the boar-hunters.

Hippocoon, -ontis, *m.,* Hippocoon.

Hippodamas, -antis, *m.,* Hippodamas, father of Perimele.

Hippothous, -i, *m.,* Hippothous, one of the boar-hunters.

hirtus, -a, -um, rough, shaggy.

holus, -eris, *n.,* cabbage.

honor, -ōris, *m.,* honour ; sacrifice, gift, reward, l. 387.

honōrātus, -a, -um, honoured, revered.

honōrō (1), honour.

hōra, -ae, *f.,* hour.

horreo, -ēre, -ui (2), stand on end, bristle.

horreum, -i, *n.,* barn.

horridus, -a, -um, bristly, bristling.

hortor (1 *dep.***).** encourage, urge, exhort.

hortus, -i, *m.,* garden.

hospes, -itis, *m.,* stranger, guest.

hostīlis, -e, of an enemy, hostile, enemy's.

hostis, -is, *c.,* enemy.

hūc, hither.

humilis, -e, low.

humus, -i, *f.,* ground ; *loc.,* **humi,** on the ground.

Hyantēus, -a, -um, of the Hyantes, *hence* Bœotian.

Hȳleūs, -ei, *m.,* Hyleus, one of the boar-hunters.

Hyperīon, -onis, *m.,* Hyperion, a name of the Sun-God.

iaceo (2), lie, lie low.

iacio, -ere, iēci, iactum, throw.

iaculum, -i, *n.,* dart, javelin.

iam, now, by now, at once ; *with* **non,** no longer.

iamdūdum, long since, this long while.

iānua, -ae, *f.,* door.

Iāson, -onis, *m.,* Jason, son of Aeson, and leader of the Argonauts.

Īcarus, -i, *m.,* Icarus, son of Daedalus.

īco, -ere, īci, ictum (3), strike.

ictus, -ūs, *m.*, blow, stroke, shot ; wound.
Īdās, -ae, *m.*, Idas, son of Aphareus.
idcirco, therefore, for that reason.
īdem, eadem, idem, the same.
iēiūnium, -i, *n.*, fast, hunger.
iēiūnus, -a, -um, fasting, hungry.
īgnārus, -a, -um, ignorant, unaware.
īgnāvus, -a, -um, idle, cowardly, shameful.
īgnis, -is, *m.*, fire.
īgnōsco, -ere, -gnōvi, -gnōtum (3), pardon (+*dat.*).
īgnōtus, -a, -um, unknown, strange.
īlia, -ium, *n. pl.*, flanks.
illāc, that way.
ille, illa, illud, that ; he, she, it, *pl.* they.
illīc, there.
illūc, thither.
imāgo, -inis, *f.*, likeness, form, semblance, sight.
imber, -bris, *m.*, rain.
imitor (1 *dep.*), imitate, feign.
immānis, -e, huge, savage, monstrous.
immemor, -oris, forgetful, heedless.
immēnsus, -a, -um, vast, measureless, bottomless.
immeritus, -a, -um, undeserving, guiltless.
immineo, -ēre (2), overhang ; be bent on (+*dat.*).
immītis, -e, cruel, ruthless.
immitto, -ere, -mīsi, -missum (3), send into, cast into.
immodicus, -a, -um, immoderate, excessive, boundless.
immūnis, -e, free from (+*gen.*).
impār, -aris, unequal, uneven.
impedio (4), hinder.
impello, -ere, -puli, -pulsum (3), push, impel, urge.
impēnsa, -ae, *f.*, spending, expense.
impero (1), order, command (+*dat.*).
(impes), impetis, *m.* =impetus.
impetus, -ūs, *m.*, attack, violence, impulse.
impietas, -ātis, *f.*, unnaturalness, lack of feeling.
impiger, -gra, -grum, active, tireless, brave.
impius, -a, -um, unnatural, lacking in natural feelings.

implacātus, -a, -um, unappeased, implacable.

impleo, -ēre, -plēvi, -plētum (2), fill, man ; fill up, make up.

implōro (1), implore.

impōno, -ere, -posui, -positum (3), put on, lay on ; put to.

imprimo, -ere, -pressi, -pressum (3), press on.

imprūdēns, -tis, unaware, ignorant.

impūne, with impunity.

īmus, -a, -um, lowest ; *used, where English prefers a noun, for* bottom ; *neut. as noun,* bottom, depth.

in, *prep. with abl.,* in, on ; *with acc.,* into, on (to), against, for.

inānis, -e, empty, vain, unsubstantial.

inattenuātus, -a, -um, undiminished.

incānus, -a, -um, grey, hoary.

incautus, -a, -um, unwary, rash.

incertus, -a, -um, uncertain, doubtful, wavering.

incīdo, -ere, -cīdi, -cīsum (3), cut into.

incipio, -ere, -cēpi, -ceptum, begin.

inclitus, -a, -um, famous, glorious.

inclūdo, -ere, -clūsi, -clūsum (3), shut in.

incola, -ae, *c.,* inhabitant.

increpo (1), chide, rail at, reproach.

incrēsco, -ere, -crēvi, -crētum (3), grow, increase *(intransitive).*

incunābula, -orum, *n. pl.* (swaddling clothes), cradle ; birthplace.

incursus, -ūs, *m.,* onset.

incurvus, -a, -um, curved.

indignor (1 *dep.*), resent (+ *dat.*).

induo, -ere, -dui, -dūtum (3), put on *(clothes).*

Indus, -a, -um, Indian.

iners, -rtis, idle, laggard ; sluggish (l. 790).

infāmia, -ae, *f.,* disgrace, shame, scandal.

infāns, -ntis, *c.,* babe.

infēlix, -īcis, unhappy, wretched, luckless.

inferiae, -arum, *f. pl.,* obsequies, sacrifices to the dead.

infestus, -a, -um, hostile.

ingenium, -i, *n.,* talent, mind, genius.

ingēns, -ntis, huge, vast, mighty.

ingrātus, -a, -um, ungrateful.

inguen, -inis, *n.*, groin.

inhaereo, -ēre, -haesi, -haesum (3), stick to, be absorbed in
  (+*dat.*).

inhibeo, -ēre, -ui, -itum (2), restrain, stay.

inhonōrātus, -a, -um, unhonoured.

inhospitus, -a, -um, inhospitable.

inimīcus, -a, -um, unfriendly, hostile.

inīquus, -a, -um, uneven, discontented.

inlino, -ere, -lēvi, -litum, smear.

innītor, -i, -nixus sum (3 *dep.*), lean on.

innumerus, -a, -um, innumerable, countless.

inops, -opis, poor, needy, destitute.

inquam, *defective verb*, say.

inrideo, -ēre, -rīsi, -rīsum (2), laugh at.

inrīto (1), provoke.

īnscius, -a, -um, ignorant.

īnsequor, -i, -secūtus sum (3 *dep.*), pursue, prosecute,
  reproach.

īnsīgnis, -e, adorned, distinguished, famed.

īnsilio, -ire, -ui (4), leap into.

īnsisto, -ere, -stiti (3), set foot on, stand on.

īnspīro (1), breathe into.

īnsto, -are, -stiti, -statum (1), stand on ; draw near, approach.

īnstruo, -ere, -ūxi, -ūctum (3), furnish, equip, provide.

īnsula, -ae, *f.*, island.

intendo, -ere, -di, -ntum, *or* -nsum (3), stretch on, stretch
  out at.

inter, *prep. with acc.*, between, among, in the midst of.

intercipio, -ere, -cēpi, -ceptum, intercept, cut off, l. 292 ; usurp.

interdum, sometimes.

intereā, meanwhile.

intervenio, -ire, -vēni, -ventum (4), come between.

intibum, -i, *n.*, endive.

intro (1), enter.

intumesco, -ere, -mui (3), swell, rise.

inultus, -a, -um, unavenged.

invenio, -ire, -vēni, -ventum (4), find.

invictus, -a, -um, unconquered.

invideo, -ēre, -vīdi, -vīsum (2), envy, grudge (+*dat*.).

invidiōsus, -a, -um, hateful, hated.

invītus, -a, -um, unwilling.

Iolāus, -i, *m.*, Iolaus.

ipse, -a, -um, self, himself, etc. ; mere.

īra, -ae, *f.*, anger.

is, ea, id, that ; he, she, it ; *pl.* they.

isset = i(v)isset.

iste, -a, -ud, that of yours, that (*you know of*) ; he, she, it, etc.

ita, thus, so.

iter, itineris, *n.*, journey, course ; path, way.

itero (1), repeat, do again ; reach again (l. 172).

iterum, again.

iubeo, -ēre, iussi, iussum (2), order, command.

iūdex, -icis, *c.*, judge.

iūdicium, -i, *n.*, judgment, verdict, decision.

iuncus, -i, *m.*, rush, reed.

iungo, -ere, -nxi, -nctum (3), join (*transitive*) ; wed.

Iūnōnius, -a, -um, of Juno, sacred to Juno.

Iuppiter, Iovis, *m.*, Jupiter, Jove.

iūro (1), swear.

iūs, iūris, *n.*, law, right, power, authority.

iustus, -a, -um, righteous, just.

iuvenālis, -e, youthful, vigorous.

iuvenca, -ae, *f.*, heifer.

iuvencus, -i, *m.*, bullock, steer.

iuvenis, -is, *m.*, youth, young man, warrior.

iuvo (1), please ; iuvat, it pleases.

iuxtā, near, close by.

Ixīon, -onis, *m.*, Ixion.

Ixīonides, -ae, *m.*, son of Ixion, i.e. Pirithous.

labefacio, -ere, -fēci, -factum, cause to totter, loosen.

lābor, -i, lāpsus sum, (3 *dep.*), slip, glide.

labor, -ōris, *m.*, labour, work, task.
lăbrum, -i, *n.*, lip.
lac, lactis, *n.*, milk.
lacer, -era, -erum, torn, mangled ; tearing (l. 877).
lacero (1), tear, rend.
lacertus, -i, *m.*, arm.
lacrima, -ae, *f.*, tear.
lacrimābilis, -e, tearful, mournful.
lacūna, -ae, *f.*, hollow, pool.
lacūno (1), panel (*verb*).
laedo, -ere, laesi, laesum (3), injure, hurt.
laetitia, -ae, *f.*, joy.
laetor (1 *dep.*), rejoice, be joyful.
laetus, -a, -um, joyful.
laeva, -ae, *f.*, left hand.
laevus, -a, -um, left.
lāmentābilis, -e, sad, mournful.
languesco, -ere, langui (3), grow weak, faint ; droop.
lapidōsus, -a, -um, stony.
lapillus, -i, *m.*, pebble.
lapis, -idis, *m.*, stone.
lapsus, -ūs, *m.*, gliding, course.
lateo, -ere, latui (2), lie hid, lurk.
latex, -icis, *m.*, liquid.
Lātōis, -idis, *f.*, daughter of Latona, *or* Leto, i.e. Diana.
Lātōnia, -ae, *f.* =Latois.
lātro (1), bark.
lātus, -a, -um, wide, broad.
laudo (1), praise.
laus, -dis, *f.*, praise, fame, merit.
Lebinthus, -i, *f.*, Lebinthus, Aegean island.
lectus, -i, *m.*, bed, couch, bier.
lego, -ere, lēgi, lectum (3), choose.
Lelegēius, -a, -um, of the Leleges.
Lelex, -egis, *m.*, Lelex.
lēnio (4), soften, appease.
lēnis, -e, soft, mild, gentle.
lēniter, softly, gently, mildly.

lentus, -a, -um, pliant, flexible, tough.
leo, -ōnis, *m.*, lion.
lētifer, -era, -erum, deadly, fatal.
Lētōius, -a, -um, of Leto *or* Latona.
lētum, -i, *n.*, death.
Leucippus, -i, *m.*, Leucippus, one of the boar-hunters.
lēvis, -e, smooth.
levis, -e, light, slight, unsubstantial.
leviter, lightly.
levo (1), raise, uplift, lighten, relieve, support.
lex, lēgis, *f.*, law, terms.
Līber, -eri, *m.*, Liber, a name of Bacchus, the wine-god.
lībo (1), pour libation, pour out wine as an offering.
libro (1), balance, poise, swing ; hurl, aim.
licet, -ēre, -uit *or* licitum est (2 *impers.*), it is allowed, is
    lawful ; *as conjunction*, although (+ *subj.*).
līgnum, -i, *n.*, wood, timber, tree.
līmen, -inis, *n.*, threshold, door.
līmes, -itis, *m.*, path, line, course.
līmōsus, -a, -um, muddy.
lingua, -ae, *f.*, tongue.
linquo, -ere, līqui (3), leave, abandon, fail.
līnum, -i, *n.*, thread.
liqueo, -ēre, licui (2), be clear.
liquidus, -a, -um, clear, flowing.
lītus, -oris, *n.*, shore.
līveo, -ēre (2), be black and blue, be bruised.
locus, -i, *m.*, place (*pl. sometimes* loca), the neighbourhood,
    the country side.
longē, far, far off.
longus, -a, -um, long.
loquor, -i, locūtus sum (3 *dep.*), speak, say.
Lūcifer, -i, *m.*, Lucifer, the morning star.
luctus, -ūs, *m.*, grief.
lūcus, -i, *m.*, wood, (sacred) grove.
lūdo, -ere, lūsi, lūsum (3), play.
lūgeo, -ēre, luxi (2), grieve.
lumbus, -i, *m.*, loin.

lūmen, -inis, *n.*, light ; eye.

lūna, -ae, *f.*, moon.

luo, -ere, lui, luitum (3), atone for, pay.

lūsus, -ūs, *m.*, play.

lux, lūcis, *f.*, light.

Lyaeus, -i, *m.*, Lyaeus (=*he who frees from care*), a name of the wine-god.

Lycaeus, -i, *m.*, Lycaeus, mountain in Arcadia; *as adj.*, l. 317, Arcadian.

Lyncēūs, -ei, *m.*, Lynceus, son of Aphareus.

lyra, -ae, *f.*, lute, lyre.

macies, -ei, *f.*, leanness, emaciation.

macto (1), sacrifice.

madefacio, -ere, -fēci, -factum, moisten, wet.

madeo, -ēre, -ui (2), be wet.

Maeandrus, *or* Maeander, -dri, *m.*, the Meander, river of Phrygia famous for its winding course.

maereo, -ēre (2), mourn.

maestus, -a, -um, sad.

māgniloquus, -a, -um, boastful.

māgnus, -a, -um, great.

māior, -ius, greater (*comp. of* māgnus).

male, badly, ill.

mālum, -i, *n.*, apple.

malum, -i, *n.*, evil.

mandātum, -i, *n.*, mission, command.

maneo, -ēre, mānsi, mānsum (2), stay, remain, wait, await.

mānes, -ium, *m. pl.*, spirits of the dead, shades.

manus, -ūs, *f.*, hand ; band.

mare, -is, *n.*, sea.

marmor, -oris, *n.*, marble.

Mars, -tis, *m.*, Mars, god of war.

massa, -ae, *f.*, lump.

māter, -tris, *f.*, mother.

māteria, -ae, *f.*, material.

māternus, -a, -um, of a mother.

mātūrus, -a, -um, ripe.

Mavors, -tis, *m.*, Mars.

Mavortius, -a, -um, of Mars, warlike.

māximus, -a, -um, greatest (*superl. of* māgnus).

mēcum = cum me.

medius, -a, -um, middle, mid ; *neut. as noun,* middle, midst.

mel, mellis, *n.*, honey.

Meleager *or* Meleagros, -gri, *m.*, Meleager.

melior, -us, better (*comp. of* bonus) ; stronger, l. 475.

melius, *adv.*, better (*comp. of* bene).

membrum, -i, *n.*, limb.

memor, -oris, mindful.

memoro (1), relate, say.

mēns, -tis, *m.*, mind, thoughts, feeling, senses.

mēnsa, -ae, *f.*, table.

mēnsis, -is, *m.*, month.

mēnsūra, -ae, *f.*, measure.

menta, -ae, *f.*, mint.

mentior (4 *dep.*), lie, say falsely.

mereo (2), deserve, earn.

mergo, -ere, -si, -sum (3), sink (*transitive*), engulf.

mergus, -i, *m.*, diver (*a kind of waterfowl*).

merito, deservedly.

meritum, -i, *n.*, service, favour ; merit, desert, fault.

merum, -i, *n.*, (unwatered) wine.

messis, -is, *f.*, harvest.

mētior, -iri, mēnsus sum (4 *dep.*), measure, traverse.

meto, -ere, messui, messum (3), reap, mow down.

metuo, -ere, -ui, -utum (3), fear.

metus, -ūs, *m.*, fear.

meus, -a, -um, my, mine.

mico, -are, -cui (1), flash.

mīles, -itis, *m.*, soldier.

mille, thousand.

mina, -ae, *f.*, threat.

Minerva, -ae, *f.*, Minerva.

L

minimus, -a, -um, smallest (*superl. of* parvus).
Mīnōis, -idis, *f.*, daughter of Minos, i.e. Ariadne.
minor (1 *dep.*), threaten.
minor, -us, smaller (*comp. of* parvus).
Mīnos, -ōis, *m.*, Minos, King of Crete.
minuo, -ere, -ui, -utum (3), make smaller ; break up small.
minus, less.
mīrābilis, -e, wonderful, wondrous.
mīror (1 *dep.*), wonder, marvel, wonder at.
mīrus, -a, -um, wondrous.
misceo, -ēre, -cui, mixtum (2), mix (*transitive*).
miser, -era, -erum, hapless, wretched.
miserābilis, -e, pitiful
misereor (2 *dep.*), pity.
mītis, -e, gentle, mild, merciful.
mitto, -ere, mīsi, missum (3), send, hurl, shoot.
moderātor, -ōris, *m.*, manager, wielder.
moderor (1 *dep.*), restrain, guide, control.
modicus, -a, -um, moderate, small.
modo, only, just, lately ; modo . . . modo, now . . . now.
modus, -i, *m.*, measure, circumference.
moenia, -ium, *n. pl.*, (city) walls, ramparts.
mōles, -is, *f.*, mass.
mōlior (4 *dep.*), set about.
mōlītcr, -ōris, *m.*, contriver.
mollio (4), make soft, soften, make supple.
mollis, -e, soft.
moneo (2), warn.
monitus, -ūs, *m.*, warning.
mōns, -tis, *m.*, mountain.
mōnstrum, -i, *n.*, monster, horror.
montānus, -a, -um, of the mountains, mountain (*as adj.*).
mora, -ae, *f.*, delay, long time.
morbus, -i, *m.*, disease.
mordeo, -ēre, momordi, morsum (2), bite ; clasp, l. 318.
morior, -i, mortuus sum (*dep.*), die.
moror (1 *dep.*), delay, hinder.
mors, -tis, *f.*, death.

morsus, -ūs, *m.*, bite.

mortālis, -e, mortal, human.

mōtus, -ūs, *m.*, movement.

moveo, -ēre, mōvi, mōtum (2), move (*transitive*) ; ply.

mox, soon, presently.

mulceo, -ēre, -si, -sum (2), stroke, caress, soothe, lull.

multicavus, -a, -um, porous.

multifidus, -a, -um, split into many pieces.

multiplex, -icis, manifold.

multus, -a, -um, much ; *in pl.*, many.

mundus, -i, *m.*, world.

mūnus, -eris, *n.*, gift.

mūrex, -icis, *m.*, purple-shell.

murmur, -uris, *n.*, murmur.

mūrus, -i, *m.*, wall.

muscus, -i, *m.*, moss.

mūto (1), change, take in exchange.

mūtuus, -a, -um, in exchange, mutual.

Nāis, -idis, *f.*, Naiad (*a water nymph*).

nam, namque, for.

nārro (1), relate, tell.

Nārycius, -a, -um, of Naryx.

nāscor, -i, nātus sum (3 *dep.*), be born.

nātālis, -e, natal, native ; *sc.* dies, birthday.

nātūra, -ae, *f.*, nature.

nātus, -a, -um (*partic. of* nascor), born ; *masc. and fem. as*
   noun, son, daughter of (+*abl.*).

nāvita, -ae, *m.*, mariner.

-ne, whether.

nē, lest, that . . . not, not.

nec, neque, and not, neither, nor, but not.

neco (1), kill, slay.

necto, -ere, -xui, -xum (3), bind, entwine.

nefandus, -a, -um, unspeakable, wicked, impious.

nefas, wickedness, sin, crime.

nego (1), deny.

nēmo, -inis, *c.*, no-one.

nempe, of course, surely.

nemus, -oris, *n.*, wood, grove, forest.

neo, -ēre, nēvi, nētum (2), spin.

Neptūnus, -i, *m.*, Neptune (*god of the sea*).

neque, *see* nec.

nequeo, -ire, -ii, -itum, be unable, cannot.

nēquīquam, in vain.

nervus, -i, *m.*, sinew, string (*of bow or catapult*).

nescio (4), not know.

nescioquis, -quid, someone, something.

Nestor, -oris, *m.*, Nestor, King of Pylos.

neu, nēve, nor, and lest.

nex, necis, *f.*, death.

nīdus, -i, *m.*, nest.

niger, -gra, -grum, black.

nīl, *n.*, nothing.

nimium, too, too much.

nimius, -a, -um, too great, excessive.

Nīsēius, -a, -um, of Nisus; virgo Nīsēia, l. 35, Scylla.

nisi, unless, if not, except.

Nīsus, -i, *m.*, Nisus, King of Megara.

nitidus, -a, -um, bright, gleaming.

nītor, -i, nīsus *or* nīxus sum (3 *dep.*), lean, toil, struggle.

nix, nivis, *f.*, snow.

no (1), swim, float.

nōbilis, -e, famous.

noceo (2), harm, injure, damage (+ *dat.*).

nōdus, -i, *m.*, knot, coil.

nōmen, -inis, *n.*, name.

nōn, not.

Nōnācrius, -a, -um, of Nonacris.

nōndum, not yet.

nōs, nostri *or* nostrum, we.

nōsco, -ere, nōvi, nōtum (3), get to know, learn; *in perf. tenses,* know.

noster, -tra, -trum, our; my.

nota, -ae, *f.*, mark.
noto (1), mark, observe.
novēnus, -a, -um, nine each.
novitas, -ātis, *f.*, newness, strangeness, novelty.
novo (1), make new, change.
novus, -a, -um, new, strange, unprecedented.
nox, -ctis, *f.*, night.
nūbes, -is, *f.*, cloud.
nūbila, -orum, *n. pl.*, clouds.
nūdo (1), bare, strip, expose.
nūdus, -a, -um, bare, naked.
nūllus, -a, -um, no, none, not any ; *as pronoun*, no-one.
nūmen, -inis, *n.*, god, divinity, divine power.
numerus, -i, *m.*, number.
numquam, never.
nunc, now.
nūper, lately, newly.
nurus, -ūs, daughter-in-law.
nūtrio (4), nourish, feed.
nūtrix, -īcis, *f.*, nurse.
nux, nucis, *f.*, nut.
nympha, -ae, *f.*, nymph.

ō, oh.
oblīquus, -a, -um, slanting, slant-wise.
oblivīscor, -i, -ītus sum (3 *dep.*), forget (+*gen.*).
obses, -idis, *c.*, hostage.
obstipesco, -ere, -pui (3), be amazed.
obsto, -are, -stiti, -statum (1), stand in the way of (+*dat.*).
obstruo, -ere, -xi, -ctum (3), block, bar, close.
occupo (1), seize on, forestall (l. 399).
occurro, -ere, -curri, -cursum (3), meet (+*dat.*).
oculus, -i, *m.*, eye.
ōdi, -isse, *defective verb*, hate.
odor, -ōris, *m.*, scent, fragrance.
odōrātus, -a, -um, scented, fragrant.

Oeclīdes, -ae, *m.*, son of Oecleus, i.e. Amphiaraus.
Oenēus, -ei, *m.*, Oeneus, King of Calydon.
Oenīdes, -ae, *m.*, son of Oeneus, i.e. Meleager.
officium, -i, *n.*, service, duty, dutifulness.
ōlim, once, formerly.
olīva, -ae, *f.*, olive.
omnis, -e, all, every.
onero (1), load.
opācus, -a, -um, dark.
operātus, -a, -um, employed in (+*dat.*).
opifex, -icis, *c.*, worker, craftsman.
opprobrium, -i, *n.*, shame, disgrace, reproach.
(ops), opis, *f.*, aid ; *in pl.*, wealth, resources.
opto (1), desire, choose.
opus, -eris, *n.*, work, task ; need.
ōra, -ae, *f.*, edge, shore, land.
orbis, -is, *m.*, circle ; world, region ; knee-cap (l. 808).
orbus, -a, -um, bereft, fatherless, childless.
ordo, -inis, *m.*, order, rank, row, line.
Orēas, -adis, *f.*, Oread (*mountain nymph*).
Orīon, -onis, *m.*, Orion.
orior, -īri, ortus sum (4 *dep.*), rise.
ōro (1), beg, pray for.
ōs, ōris, *n.*, mouth ; face, head ; *in pl.* lips, jaws.
os, ossis, *n.*, bone.
osculum, -i, *n.*, kiss.
ostendo, -ere, -di, -sum *or* -tum (3), show, display.
ostrum, -i, *n.*, purple.
ōvum, -i, *n.*, egg.

pābulum, -i, *n.*, food.
Pagasaeus, -a, -um, of Pagasae (*port in Thessaly from which
    the Argo sailed*).
Palladius, -a, -um, of Pallas.
Pallas, -adis, *f.*, Pallas (=Minerva).
palleo (2), be pale.

pallesco, -ere, pallui (3), grow pale, fade.

pallor, -ōris, *m.*, pallor, paleness.

Pallor, -ōris, *m.*, Pallor *(personified)*.

palma, -ae, *f.*, palm, hand ; date (l. 674).

palmes, -itis, *m.*, vine-shoot.

palūs, -ūdis, *f.*, marsh.

palūster, -tris, -tre, of the marsh, marshy.

pando, -ere, pandi, passum (3), open, spread, fling wide.

Panopeus, -ei, *m.*, Panopeus, one of the boar-hunters.

pār, paris, equal, even, like.

parātus, -ūs, *m.*, preparation, magnificence.

Parcae, -arum, *f. pl.*, the Parcae, the Fates.

parēns, -ntis, *c.*, parent, father, mother.

pāreo (2), obey (+*dat.*).

parīlis, -e, equal, like.

pario, -ere, peperi, partum, bear, produce.

pariter, equally, alike, at the same time.

paro (1), prepare, procure, buy.

Paros, -i, *f.*, Paros, Aegean island.

Parrhasius, -a, -um, Parrhasian *(from district in Arcadia)*.

pars, -tis, *f.*, part, side, share ; some.

Parthāonius, -a, -um, of Parthaon.

partus, -ūs, *m.*, birth ; young, offspring.

parum, too little.

parvus, -a, -um, small; humble, l. 637.

pāsco, -ere, pāvi, pāstum (3), feed.

passus, -a, -um, *partic. of* pando, dishevelled, disordered.

pastor, -ōris, *m.*, shepherd.

pateo, -ēre, -ui (2), be open, stand revealed.

pater, -tris, *m.*, father.

paternus, -a, -um, of a father.

patior, -i, passus sum *(dep.)*, bear, suffer.

patria, -ae, *f.*, native land, country.

patrius, -a, -um, father's, native.

patulus, -a, -um, broad, spreading.

pauci, -ae, -a, few.

paulātim, little by little, gradually.

paulum, a little.

pauper, -eris, poor.

paupertas, -ātis, *f.*, poverty.

paveo, -ēre, pāvi (2), fear, dread, be horrified at.

pax, pācis, *f.*, peace.

pectus, -oris, *n.*, breast.

pecus, -ūdis, *f.*, beast, animal.

Pelagōn, -ōnis, *m.*, Pelagon, one of the boar-hunters.

pelagus, -i, *n.*, sea.

Pēleus, -ei, *m.*, Peleus.

Pelopēius, -a, -um, of Pelops.

Penātes, -um, *m. pl.*, household gods ; house, home.

pendeo, -ēre, pependi (2), hang, hover, be in the balance, l. 12 ; hang over, hang free *or* unsupported.

pendo, -ere, pependi, pēnsum (3), weigh ; pay.

Pēnelope, *or* Pēnelopa, -es *or* -ae, Penelope, wife of Ulysses.

penetrāle, -is, *n.*, inmost part.

penna, -ae, *f.*, feather, wing.

per, *prep. with acc.*, through, over, along.

perago, -ere, -ēgi, -āctum (3), fulfil, carry out, accomplish.

percipio, -ere, -cēpi, -ceptum, gather, collect, catch.

perdix, -īcis, *c.*, partridge.

perdo, -ere, -didi, -ditum (3), destroy.

peregrīnus, -a, -um, foreign, coming from afar.

perennis, -e, lasting, perpetual.

pereo, -ire, -ii, -itum, perish.

perīclum *or* perīculum, -i, *n.*, danger.

Perimele, -es, *f.*, Perimele.

perimo, -ere, -ēmi, -emptum (3), destroy.

perisset = peri(v)isset.

perōdi, -isse, *defective verb*, loathe, detest.

perpetuus, -a, -um, lasting, continuous, uninterrupted.

persequor, -i, -secūtus sum (3 *dep.*), follow up, persist in; set forth, relate.

pervenio, -ire, -vēni, -ventum (4), come to, arrive, reach.

pervius, -a, -um, passable.

pēs, pedis, *m.*, foot.

pestifer, -era, -erum, deadly, baneful.

peto, -ere, -ī(v)i, -ītum (3), seek, ask, make for, aim at, pelt.

pharetra, -ae, *f.*, quiver.
Pherētiades, -ae, *m.*, son of Pheres, i.e. Admetus.
Philēmon, -onis, *m.*, Philemon.
Phoebus, -i, *m.*, Phoebus, the sun-god, and god of archery and poetry.
Phoenix, -icis, *m.*, Phoenix.
Phrygius, -a, -um, Phrygian.
Phȳlēus, -ei, *m.*, Phyleus, one of the boar-hunters.
piētas, -ātis, *f.*, natural affection.
pīgnus, -oris, *n.*, pledge ; child.
pingo, -ere, -nxi, -ctum (3), paint ; embroider.
pio (1), expiate, atone *(for)*.
Pirithous, -i, *m.*, Pirithous, companion of Theseus.
piscis, -is, *m.*, fish.
Pitthēus, -ei, *m.*, Pittheus.
pius, -a, -um, loving, filial, etc., *masc. pl.* pii (l. 724) the good, good people.
placeo (2), please (+*dat.*)
placidus, -a, -um, calm, gentle, mild.
plango, -ere, -nxi, -nctum (3), strike, beat.
plangor, -ōris, *m.*, beating the breast, lamentation.
plānus, -a, -um, level, flat ; *neut. as noun,* level ground.
plaudo, -ere, -si, -sum (3), clap, strike, flap.
plēnus, -a, -um, full.
Plexippus, -i, *m.*, Plexippus.
plūma, -ae, *f.*, feather.
plūrimus, most *(superl. of* multus).
plūs, plūris, more *(comp. of* multus).
plūs, *adv.*, more.
pluviālis, -e, of rain, rainy.
pōculum, -i, *n.*, drinking cup, goblet.
poena, -ae, *f.*, penalty, punishment.
pollex, -icis, *m.*, thumb.
pondus, -eris, *n.*, weight.
pōno, -ere, posui, positum (3), put, place, set, set up, set before, build ; serve up ; lay, lay down *or* aside, doff.
pontus, -i, *m.*, sea.
poples, -itis, *m.*, back of the knee.

populus, -i, *m.*, people, nation.
porrigo, -ere, -rexi, -rectum (3), stretch out, extend.
porta, -ae, *f.*, gate.
portus, -ūs, *m.*, harbour.
posco, -ere, poposci (3), ask, demand.
possideo, -ēre, -sēdi, -sessum (2), be master of, own, possess.
possum, posse, potui, can, be able, may.
post, *prep. with acc.*, after.
postis, -is, *m.*, post, door-post ; door.
postquam, after, when.
potēns, -tis, powerful, master of.
potentia, -ae, *f.*, power.
potestas, -ātis, *f.*, power.
potior (4 *dep.*), obtain (+*abl. or gen.*).
potius, rather.
praebeo (2), offer, give.
praeceps, -cipitis, headlong.
praeceptum, -i, *n.*, teaching, instruction.
praecipuē, chiefly, especially.
praecordia, -orum, *n. pl.*, heart.
praeda, -ae, *f.* booty, spoil, prey.
praefero, -ferre, -tuli, -lātum, place before, prefer.
praemium, -i, *n.*, reward, prize.
praesto, -are, -stiti, -stitum (1), excel (+*dat.*), fulfil, give.
praetempto (1), try beforehand, make trial of first.
praetendo, -ere, -di, -tum (3), stretch forward, hold in front.
praeter, *prep. with acc.*, beyond, besides, except.
praetereo, -ire, -i(v)i, -itum, pass over, pass by.
precor (1 *dep.*), pray.
premo, -ere, pressi, pressum (3), press, crush, sit on, l. 34 ;
  tread ; spurn.
presso (1), press.
pretiōsus, -a, -um, precious.
(prex, precis), *f.*, prayer, entreaty.
prīmitiae, -arum, *f. pl.*, first fruits.
prīmum, *adv.*, first.
prīmus, -a, -um, first ; early, l. 313.
prior, -us, former, earlier, previous, first (*of two*).

pro, *prep. with abl.*, for, on behalf of, instead of.

probo (1), test, try, approve.

procer, -eris, *m.*, chief.

procul, far, from afar.

prōculco (1), tread down, trample under foot.

prōdeo, -ire, -i(v)i, -itum, go forth, project.

prōditio, -ōnis, *f.*, treachery.

prōdo, -ere, -didi, -ditum (3), betray.

prōdūco, -ere, -dūxi, -dūctum (3), draw out, bring forth, bring.

profānus, -a, -um, not sacred, impious.

profecto, surely.

prōfero, -ferre, -tuli, -lātum, bring forth.

profundo, -ere, -fūdi, -fūsum (3), pour out.

profundus, -a, -um, deep ; *neut. as noun*, the deep, the sea.

prōgenies, -ēi, *f.*, offspring.

prōgigno, -ere, -genui, -genitum (3), beget.

prohibeo (2), forbid, prevent.

prōles, -is, *f.*, offspring, brood.

prōmitto, -ere, -mīsi, -missum (3), promise.

prōnus, -a, -um, downward, on the face.

prōpello, -ere, -puli, -pulsum (3), drive forward *or* forth, cast down.

propero (1), hasten.

propter, *prep. with acc.*, near ; on account of.

prospicio, -ere, -spexi, -spectum, look out, look on, see.

prosterno, -ere, -strāvi, -strātum (3), throw down.

prōsum, prōdesse, prōfui, be of advantage to, avail (+*dat.*).

prōtego, -ere, -xi, -ctum (3), protect.

Protēūs, -ei, *m.*, Proteus, a sea-god, gifted with the power of assuming various shapes.

prōtinus, forthwith.

prōvolvo, -ere, -volvi, -volutum (3) roll forward, roll along (*transitive*).

proximus, -a, -um, nearest, next.

prūna, -ae, *f.*, ember.

prūnum, -i, *n.*, plum.

pudor, -ōris, *m.*, shame, modesty ; disgrace, blot.

puer, -i, *m.*, boy.
puerīlis, -e, boyish.
pūgno (1), fight, be at war.
pulcher, -chra, -chrum, beautiful.
pulvis, -eris, *m.*, dust.
pūmex, -icis, pumice(-stone).
puppis, -is, *f.*, stern, ship.
purpura, -ae, *f.*, purple, the purple lock (l. 80).
purpureus, -a, -um, purple, robed in purple.
puto (1), think.
Pylius, -a, -um, of Pylos, Pylian, i.e. Nestor, l. 365.

quā, where, so far as.
quaero, -ere, -sīvi, -sītum (3), seek, ask for.
quālis, -e, such as, as.
quam, than.
quamquam, although, though.
quamvīs, although, though.
quantus, -a, -um, how great, how much ; *rel.*, as much as.
quātenus, as far as, since (l. 784).
quater, four times.
quatio, -ere, ——, quassum (3), shake (*transitive*).
-que, and, both.
quercus, -ūs, *f.*, oak.
quernus, -a, -um, of an oak, oak (*as adj.*).
queror, -i, questus sum (3 *dep.*), complain, complain of.
qui, quae, quod, *rel. pron.*, who, which ; *interrog. adj.*, what ? which ?
quicumque, quaecumque, quodcumque, whoever, whatever.
quid, why ?
quidem, indeed.
quies, -ētis, *f.*, sleep, repose, rest.
quīnque, five.
quis, quae, quid, *interrog. pron.*, who ? what ?
quis, quid, *indef. pron.*, anyone, anything (*after* si, num, nisi, ne).

quisque, quaeque, quidque (*as adj.*, *neut.* quodque), each.

quisquis, quicquid (*as adj.*, *neut.* quodquod), whoever, whatever.

quō, whither, to which, into which ; *with comparatives*, the, e.g. quo senior fit, ' *the* older he grows '.

quō, in order that (*with comparatives*).

quod, because, the fact that.

quondam, formerly, sometimes.

quoniam, since (*causal*).

quoque, also, even.

quot, as many as.

rādix, -īcis, *f.*, root.

rāmāle, -is, *n.*, stick.

rāmus, -i, *m.*, branch.

rapax, -ācis, grasping, greedy.

rapidus, -a, -um, fierce, scorching ; swift.

rapio, -ere, rapui, raptum, seize, carry off *or* away ; hurry.

rapto (1), carry off, drag away.

raptor, -ōris, *m.*, robber.

rārus, -a, -um, scattered.

rāsilis, -e, scraped, polished.

ratis, -is, *f.*, raft, bark, ship.

raucus, -a, -um, hoarse.

recalfacio, -ere, -fēci, -factum, warm up again, make warm again.

recēdo, -ere, -cessi, -cessum (3), retire ; lie withdrawn *or* aloof (l. 590).

recēns, -tis, fresh, new, renewed.

recipio, -ere, -cēpi, -ceptum, receive.

reclūdo, -ere, -clūsi, -clusum (3), open.

recurvus, -a, -um, curved.

recūso (1), refuse.

reddo, -ere, -didi, -ditum (3), restore, give back ; answer ; render, make.

redeo, -ire, -i(v)i, -itum, go back, return.

redoleo (2), be fragrant.
refero, -ferre, rettuli, -latum, bring back, report, tell.
rēfert, *impers.*, it matters.
refluo, -ere (3), flow back.
refoveo, -ēre, -fōvi, -fōtum (2), warm anew.
refugio, -ere, -fūgi, flee back, shrink from.
rēgia, -ae, *f.*, palace.
regio, -ōnis, *f*, region, quarter, direction.
rēgius, -a, -um, royal, of the palace.
rēgno (1), rule.
rēgnum, -i, *n.*, kingdom, realm.
rego, -ere, -xi, -ctum (3), rule, govern, manage, guide.
relego, -ere, -lēgi, -lectum (3), gather up again.
relevo (1), lift up, rest.
relinquo, -ere, -līqui, -lictum (3), leave.
remaneo, -ēre, -nsi (2), remain.
rēmex, -igis, *m.*, rower.
rēmigium, -i, *n.*, oarage.
removeo, -ēre, -mōvi, -mōtum (2), remove.
rēmus, -i, *m.*, oar.
renīdeo, -ēre (2), shine, smile.
renovāmen, -inis, *n.*, renewal, new form.
renuo, -ere, -ui (3), deny, refuse.
reperio, -īre, repperi, repertum (4), find, find out.
repeto, -ere, -petīvi, petītum (3), seek anew, repeat, retrace.
repleo, -ēre, -ēvi, -ētum (2), fill again.
repūgno (1), fight against, oppose, resist.
requies, -ētis, *f.*, rest.
requīro, -ere, -quīsīvi, -quīsītum (3), seek, ask for.
rēs, rei, *f.*, thing, matter, affair ; (l. 792), food.
reseco, -are, -cui, -ctum (1), cut off.
resequor, -i, -secūtus sum (3), answer.
resero (1), unlock, open.
resolvo, -ere, -vi, -utum (3), loosen, break.
resono (1), resound, sound.
respicio, -ere, -spexi, -spectum, look back, look back at.
respondeo, -ēre, -di, -sum (2), answer, reply.
resto, -are, -stiti (1), remain.

resurgo, -ere, -surrexi, -surrectum (3), rise again.
resuscito (1), rouse again, revive.
rēte, -is, *n.*, net.
retego, -ere, -xi, -ctum (3), uncover, reveal.
retināculum, -i, *n.*, mooring-cable, hawser.
retineo, -ēre, -tinui, -tentum (2), hold back, stop.
retro, *adv.*, back.
revello, -ere, -velli *or* -vulsi, -vulsum (3), tear away.
revertor, -i, reversus sum (3 *dep.*), return, turn round.
rēx, rēgis, *m.*, king.
rigeo, -ēre, -ui (2), be stiff, bristle.
rigidus, -a, -um, stiff, stern ; frozen.
riguus, -a, -um, well watered.
rīpa, -ae, *f.*, bank.
rivus, -i, *m.*, stream.
rōbur, -oris, *n.*, oak, timber ; strength.
rogo (1), ask.
rogus, -i, *m.* (*funeral*) pyre.
rostrum, -i, *n.*, beak, snout, muzzle ; (l. 371), tusk.
rubefacio, -ere, -fēci, -factum, make red.
rūbīgo, -inis, *f.*, rust ; (l. 802), scurf.
rubor, -ōris, *m.*, redness.
rudis, -e, raw, rough, coarse.
rugōsus, -a, -um, shrivelled, dried, wrinkled.
ruīna, -ae, *f.*, downfall, ruin.
ruo, -ere, rui (3), rush.
rursus, again.
rūs, rūris, *n.*, country.
rusticus, -a, -um, rural, rustic.

sacer, -cra, -crum, sacred, holy.
sacerdos, -ōtis, *m.*, priest.
sacrilegus, -a, -um, sacrilegious, impious.
sacrum, -i, *n.*, rite, sacrifice.
saeclum, *or* saeculum, -i, *n.*, age.
saepe, often.

saepes, -is, *f.*, hedge, fence.

saeta, -ae, *f.*, bristle.

saetiger, -era, -erum, bristle-bearing, bristly ; *masc. as noun,* boar.

saevio (4), rage.

saevus, -a, -um, cruel.

sagax, -ācis, wise, prophetic.

sagitta, -ae, *f.*, arrow.

salīgnus, -a, -um, of willow.

salix, -icis, *f.*, willow.

Samos, -i, *f.*, Samos, island off the coast of Asia Minor.

sanguis, -inis, *m.*, blood.

sānus, -a, -um, sound.

sat, *or* satis, *adv. and noun (indeclinable)*, enough.

satio (1), glut, sate, satisfy.

Sāturnius, -a, -um, of Saturn ; son of Saturn, i.e. Jupiter.

satus, -a, -um, *partic. of* sero, sprung (from), child (of) (+*abl.*)

saxum, -i, *n.*, rock, stone.

scaber, -bra, -brum, rough, scurfy.

scelerātus, -a, -um, wicked, impious.

scelus, -eris, *n.*, crime.

scindo, -ere, scidi, scissum (3), cut, tear, rend.

scopulus, -i, *m.*, rock, cliff.

Scylla, -ae, *f.*, Scylla, daughter of Nisus.

Scythia, -ae, *f.*, Scythia (*answering to Rumania and South Russia*).

sē, sui, *reflex. pron.*, himself, herself, itself ; themselves.

seco, -are, -cui, -ctum (1), cut.

sēcum = cum sē.

secundus, -a, -um, following, favourable.

secūris, -is, *f.*, axe.

secus, otherwise.

sed, but.

sedeo, -ēre, sēdi, sessum (2), sit.

sedīle, -is, *n.*, seat.

sēdūco, -ere, -dūxi, -dūctum (3), draw aside, put aside.

sēdulus, -a, -um, busy.

seges, -etis, *f.*, crop.
semel, once.
semper, always.
senecta, -ae, *f.*, old age.
senex, senis, *m.*, old man ; *sometimes as adj.*, old.
senīlis, -e, of an old man.
senior, older (*comparative of* senex, *but sometimes almost in same meaning*).
sententia, -ae, *f.*, opinion, resolve.
sentio, -īre, sēnsi, sēnsum (4), feel, perceive.
sēni, -ae, -a, six each ; (l. 243), six.
sepelio, -īre, -i(v)i, sepultum (4), bury.
sepulchrālis, -e, of the tomb, funeral.
sepulchrum, -i, *n.*, tomb.
sequor, -i, secūtus sum (3 *dep.*), follow.
sera, -ae, *f.*, bolt, bar.
sermo, -ōnis, *m.*, converse, discourse.
sero, -ere, sēvi, satum (3), sow, beget.
serpēns, -tis, *c.*, snake.
serra, -ae, *f.*, saw.
sertum, -i, *n.*, garland.
servo (1), keep, preserve, guard.
seu, whether, or ; (ll. 25, 26), if.
sextus, -a, -um, sixth.
si, if.
sīc, so, thus.
sicco (1), dry.
siccus, -a, -um, dry.
Siculus, -a, -um, Sicilian.
sīdus, -eris, *n.*, star.
sīgno (1), mark.
sīgnum, -i, *n.*, mark, track.
silva, -ae, *f.*, forest, wood.
similis, -e, like.
simplex, -icis, simple, plain, unadorned.
simul, at the same time, together ; as soon as.
simulac, as soon as.
sincērus, -a, -um, pure, virgin.

M

sine, *prep. with abl.*, witnout.
sino, -ere, sīvi, situm (3), allow.
sinuo (1), bend (*transitive*).
sīquis, if anyone ; whoever.
sisto, -ere, stiti (3), place, set.
situs, -ūs, *m.*, neglect, disuse.
socer, -eri, *m.*, father-in-law.
socius, -a, *c.*, partner, comrade.
sociātus, -a, -um, shared, common.
sōl, sōlis, *m.*, sun.
sōlācium, -i, *n.*, solace, comfort.
soleo, -ēre, solitus sum (2 *semi-dep.*), be accustomed.
solidus, -a, -um, solid, strong.
solitus, -a, -um, wonted, accustomed.
sollicitus, -a, -um, anxious.
solum, -i, *n.*, soil, ground, place.
sōlum, only.
sōlus, -a, -um, alone.
solvo -ere, -vi, -ūtum (3), loosen, weaken, melt, relax ;
    pay.
somnus, -i, *m.*, sleep.
sono, -are. -ui, -itum (1), sound.
sonus, -i, *m.*, sound, voice.
sopor, -ōris, *m.*, sleep, slumber.
sordidus, -a, -um, dirty, smoky.
soror, -ōris, *f.*, sister.
sors, -tis, *f.*, lot, portion, casting lots.
sortior (4 *dep.*), obtain by lot.
spargo, -ere, -rsi, -rsum (3), scatter, spread, sprinkle.
spatiōsus, -a, -um, roomy, spacious ; long, l. 580.
spatium, -i, *n.*, distance.
species, -ēi, *f.*, sight, shape, form.
specto (1), watch, behold ; test, try.
sperno, -ere, sprēvi, sprētum (3), scorn, despise.
spēro (1), hope.
spēs, ei, *f.*, hope.
spīca, -ae, *f.*, ear of corn.
spīculum, -i, *n.*, point.

spīna, -ae, *f.*, thorn ; back-bone.

spīritus, -ūs, *m.*, breath.

spīro (1), breathe.

splendidus, -a, -um, shining, bright.

spolio (1), rob, strip, despoil.

spolium, -i, *n.*, spoil, prize.

sponda, -ae, *f.*, frame (*of a bed*).

sponte, of one's own accord.

sprētor, -ōris, *m.*, despiser.

spūma, -ae, *f.*, foam.

spūmo (1), foam.

stabulum, -i, *n.*, stall, fold.

stāgnum, -i, *n.*, pool, swamp.

stāmen, -inis, *n.*, warp, thread.

sterilis, -e, barren.

sterno, -ere, strāvi, strātum (3) lay low, spread.

stīpes, -itis, *m.*, billet, faggot, brand.

stīpula, -ae, *f.*, stalk, straw.

stīva, -ae, *f.*, plough-handle.

sto, -are, steti, statum (1), stand ; be fixed.

strāmen, -inis, *n.*, straw.

strātum, -i, *n.*, coverlet, covering.

strīdeo, -ēre (2), *or* strīdo, -ere (3), hiss.

strīdor, -ōris, *m.*, hissing.

stringo, -ere, -nxi, -ctum (3), draw ; strip, trim.

struo, -ere, -ūxi, -ūctum (3), build.

studium, -i, *n.*, desire, eagerness ; business, pursuit.

suādeo, -ēre, -āsi, -āsum (2), advise, urge, prompt, persuade.

sub, *prep. with abl.*, under, below.

subdo, -ere, -didi, -ditum (3), put under.

subeo, -īre, -i(v)i, -itum, go under, enter ; succeed, take the place of.

subicio, -ere, -iēci, -iectum, set beneath ; *in pass.*, lie beneath, l. 574.

sublīmis, -e, on high ; *neut. as noun*, height.

subveho, -ere, -xi, -ctum (3), bring up, bear aloft.

succēdo, -ere, -cessi, -cessum (3), come under, enter.

succendo, -ere, -di, -sum (3), kindle, set fire to.

successus, -ūs, *m.*, victory, success, triumph.
succīdo, -ere, -cīdi, -cīsum (3), fell.
succingo, -ere, -nxi, -nctum (3), gird up, tuck up.
succrēsco, -ere, -ēvi (3), grow up, rise up.
sufficio, -ere, -fēci, -fectum, suffice.
sum, esse, fui, be.
summitto, -ere, -mīsi, -missum (3), let down, lower, stoop.
summoveo, -ēre, -mōvi, -mōtum (2), drive away.
summus, -a, -um, highest, top, top of.
sūmo, -ere, -mpsi, -mptum (3), take, take up ; put on.
super, *prep. with acc.*, above, over, upon ; in addition to.
superi, -orum, *m. pl.*, the gods (*above*).
superinicio, -ere, -iēci, -iectum, cast on, fling on.
supero (1), overcome.
supīnus, -a, -um, face upwards, upturned, thrown back.
supplex, -icis, *m.*, suppliant.
suprēmus, -a, -um, highest, last.
surgo, -ere, -rexi, -rectum (3), rise, ascend.
sūs, suis, *c.*, pig.
suscito (1), rouse, wake, stir up.
suspēnsus, -a, -um, hung up, suspended, lifted up.
sustineo, -ēre, -tinui, -tentum (2), hold up ; (l. 500), endure.
suus, -a, -um, his, her, its, their (*own*) ; master of oneself.
Syrtis, -is, *f.*, Syrtis.

tabella, -ae, *f.*, tablet.
tabeo, -ēre, -bui (2), melt (*intransitive*).
taceo (2), be silent.
taciturnus, -a, -um, silent.
taeda, -ae, *f.*, torch, brand, faggot.
tālis, -e, such.
tālus, -i, *m.*, ankle.
tam, so.
tamen, yet, however, nevertheless.
tandem, at last.
tango, -ere, tetigi, tactum (3),touch, reach, set foot on.

tantum, as much ; only.

tantummodo, only.

tantus, -a, -um, so great.

tardus, -a, -um, slow.

taurus, -i, *m.,* bull.

tectum, -i, *n.,* roof ; dwelling, house.

tēcum = cum tē.

Tegeaeus, -a, -um, of Tegea, Tegean ; *in fem.,* she of Tegea i.e. Atalanta.

tego, -ere, texi, tectum (3), cover, hide.

Telamōn, -ōnis, *m.,* Telamon.

tellūs, -ūris, *f.,* earth, ground, land.

tēlum, -i, *n.,* spear ; weapon.

temerārius, -a, -um, rash, reckless.

temero (1), defile, violate.

templum, -i, *n.,* temple.

tempus, -oris, *n.,* time, season ; *in pl.,* temples (*of the head*).

tendo, -ere, tetendi, tentum (3), stretch.

tenebrae, -arum, *f. pl.,* darkness, gloom.

teneo, -ēre, -ui, tentum (2), hold, occupy ; check, detain ; maintain, support; reach (*a place*).

tener, -era, -erum, soft, tender, frail, young.

tentōrium, -i, *n.,* tent.

tenuis, -e, thin, slight, small.

tepidus, -a, -um, warm.

ter, thrice.

tergeo, -ēre, tersi, tersum (2), wipe.

tergum, -i, *or* **tergus, -oris,** *n.,* back, chine ; hide, skin.

tero, -ere, trīvi, trītum (3), rub.

terra, -ae, *f.,* earth, land, country ;   **orbis terrarum, the** world.

terreo (2), frighten.

tertius, -a, -um, third.

testa, -ae, *f.* tile, potsherd.

testor (1 *dep.*), bear witness, prove.

textum, -i, *n.,* thing woven, stuff.

thalamus, -i, *m.,* chamber ; wedlock.

Thēseūs, -ei, *m.,* Theseus.

Thēsēus, -a, -um, of Theseus.

Thessalus, -a, -um, Thessalian.

Thestiades, -ae, *m.*, son of Thestius, i.e. Plexippus *or* Toxeus.

Thestias, -adis, *f.*, daughter of Thestius, i.e. Althaea.

Thestius, -i, *m.*, Thestius.

Thynēius, -a, -um, Bithynian.

tīgnum, -i, *n.*, beam.

tigris, -idis, *c.*, tiger, tigress.

tilia, -ae, *f.*, lime-tree, linden.

timeo (2), fear.

timidus, -a, -um, fearful, timid.

titulus, -i, *m.*, inscription, honour.

tollo, -ere, sustuli, sublātum (3), lift, take away.

tondeo, -ēre, totondi, tōnsum (2), shear, remove.

tōphus, -i, *m.*, tufa (*stone*).

torqueo, -ēre, -si, -tum (2), twist, hurl.

torrēns, -ntis, *m.*, torrent.

torreo, -ēre, -ui, tostum (2), roast, scorch, burn.

torris, -is, *m.*, brand.

torus, -i, *m.*, couch, bed, mattress.

totidem, (just) as *or* so many.

totiēns, so often.

tōtus, -a, -um, whole.

Toxēus, -ei, *m.*, Toxeus.

trabs, -bis, *f.*, beam, plank.

tracto (1), handle.

trādo, -ere, -didi, -ditum (3), hand over, give (up), sur-render.

traho, -ere, -āxi, -āctum (3), draw, drag, drag along, carry away, turn; take, l. 230.

trānseo, -īre, -i(v)i, -itum, pass.

trānsformis, -e, changed, capable of changing its shape.

tremo, -ere, -ui (3), tremble.

Tremor, -ōris, *m.*, Trembling (*personified*).

tremulus, -a, -um, trembling, quivering.

trepido (1), hurry.

tribūtum, -i, *n.*, tax, tribute.

Tridentifer, -i, *m.,* bearer of the trident, i.e. Neptune.

Triopēĭs, -idis, *f.,* daughter of Triopas.

Triopēius, -a, -um, *(son)* of Triopas.

triplex, -icis, threefold, three.

trīstis, -e, sad, mournful.

Trītōnis, -idis, *f.,* Minerva (name taken from her birth-place).

Troezēnius, -a, -um, of Troezen.

Troiānus, -a, -um, of Troy, Trojan.

trunco (1), mutilate, strip.

truncus, -i, *m.,* (tree)-trunk.

trux, -cis, grim, fierce, savage.

tū, tui, thou, you.

tūber, -is, *n.,* hump, lump, swelling.

tueor *(2 dep.),* protect, watch over, guard, keep, tend.

tum, then.

tumeo (2), swell.

tumidus, -a, -um, swelling, boastful, proud.

tumulo (1), bury.

tumulus, -i, *m.,* mound, tomb.

tunc, then.

tundo, -ere, tutudi, tunsum (3), beat.

turba, -ae, *f.,* crowd, quantity.

turbineus, -a, -um, whirling, eddying.

turbo (1), disturb, trouble, confuse, disorder.

turris, -is, *f.,* tower.

tūs, tūris, *n.,* incense.

tūtēla, -ae, *f.,* care, charge, guardianship.

tūtor, -ōris, *m.,* guardian.

tūtus, -a, -um, safe.

tuus, -a, -um, thy, your.

Tyndarides, -ae, *m.,* son of Tyndareus, i.e. Castor *or* Pollux.

ubi, where, when.

ulciscor, -i, ultus sum (3 dep.), avenge.

ūllus, -a, -um, any.

ulna, -ae, *f.*, elbow, arm ; ell.
ultimus, -a, -um, last.
ultor, -ōris, *m.*, avenger.
ulva, -ae, *f.*, sedge.
umbra, -ae, *f.*, shade.
umerus, -i, *m.*, shoulder.
ūmidus, -a, -um, damp, wet, moist.
umquam, ever.
ūnā, *adv.*, together.
unda, -ae, *f.*, wave.
unguis, -is, *m.*, nail.
ūnicus, -a, -um, sole, only.
unus, -a, -um, one, alone.
urbs, -bis, *f.*, city.
urgueo, -ēre, ursi (2), press, be pressing.
ūro, -ere, ussi, ustum (3), burn (*transitive*).
ūsus, -ūs, *m.*, use, help.
ut, in order that ; so that ; *with indic.*, as, when.
uterque, -traque, -trumque, each (of two), both.
uterus, -i, *m.*, womb.
ūtilis, -e, useful, profitable.
utinam, would that!
ūtor, -i, ūsus sum (3 *dep.*), use, experience.
ūva, -ae, *f.*, grape.

vacuus, -a, -um, empty.
vagus, -a, -um, roving, wandering.
vale, *imperative*, farewell.
valeo (2), be strong *or* well, be able.
validus, -a, -um, strong.
vallis, -is, *f.*, valley, vale.
vānus, -a, -um, empty, vain, false.
vario (1), change, vary.
varius, -a, -um, various, divers.
vāsto (1), lay waste.
vāticinor (1 *dep.*), foretell.

-ve, or, either.

vecto (1), carry, bear ; *in pass.*, ride.

vel, or.

vello, -ere, velli, vulsum (3), tear.

vēlo (1), shroud, cover, clothe.

vēlox, -ōcis, swift, quick.

vēlum, -i, *n.*, sail ; **vēla dare**, set sail.

velut, as, like.

vēna, -ae, *f.*, vein.

vēnābulum, -i, *n.*, hunting-spear.

vēndo, -ere, -didi, -ditum (3), sell.

venia, -ae, *f.*, pardon.

venio, -īre, vēni, ventum (4), come.

venter, -tris, *m.*, belly, stomach.

ventus, -i, *m.*, wind.

verbum, -i, *n.*, word.

vērē, truly, rightly.

vērō, but, indeed.

verso (1), turn, writhe.

vertex, -icis, *m.*, head ; whirlpool, eddy.

verto, -ere, -ti, -sum (3), turn, change *(transitive)*.

vērum, but.

vērus, -a, -um, true, real.

vester, -tra, -trum, your.

vestigium, -i, *n.*, footprint, *or* -step, track ; sole, foot.

vestis, -is, *f.*, garment, robe ; coverlet.

veto, -āre, -ui, -itum (1), forbid.

vetus, veteris, old.

vetustus, -a, -um, old, ancient.

via, -ae, *f.*, way, road.

vibro (1), brandish, shake ; quiver.

———, **vicis,** *f.* (*no nom. in use*) change ; **per vices**, by turns.

vīcīnia, -ae, *f.*, neighbourhood, nearness ; *as collective*, the neighbours.

vīcīnus, -a, -um, near, neighbouring.

victima, -ae, *f.*, victim.

victor, -ōris, *m.*, conqueror ; *as adj.*, triumphant, victorious.

victōria, -ae, *f.*, victory ; **Victōria**, Victory *(personified)*.

victrix, -īcis, *f.*, victorious.

video, -ēre, vīdi, vīsum (2), see ; *in pass.*, seem, appear.

vigeo, -ēre, -ui (2), be strong.

vigor, -ōris, *m.*, force, vigour, strength.

vīlis, -e, cheap, mean.

villa, -ae, *f.*, country-house, farm.

vīmen, -inis, *n.*, osier, wattle.

vincio, -īre, -nxi, -nctum (4), bind, tie, fasten.

vinco, -ere, vīci, victum (3), conquer.

vinculum, -i, *n.*, fastening, leash.

vindex, -icis, *c.*, avenger, champion.

vīnum, -i, *n.*, wine.

violentus, -a, -um, violent, furious.

violo (1), defile, violate, profane, pollute.

vir, -i, *m.*, man, hero, husband.

vireo, -ēre, -ui (3), be green.

virgineus, -a, -um, of a maiden, maiden *or* virgin, *as adj.*

virginitas, -tātis, *f.*, virginity.

virgo, -inis, *f.*, maiden.

virīlis, -e, of a man.

virtūs, -ūtis, *f.*, courage, valour, merit, worth.

vīs, vim, vi ; *pl.*, **vīres, -ium,** *f.*, ; *sg.* force, violence ; *pl.* strength.

viscus, -eris, *n.*, *usually in pl.*, entrails, vitals. organs ; flesh, flesh and blood.

vīta, -ae, *f.*, life.

vītālis, -e, of life, vital.

vītis, -is, *f.*, vine.

vitta, -ae, *f.*, fillet, chaplet.

vīvo, -ere, vixi, victum (3), live.

vīvus, -a, -um, living, alive.

vix, scarcely, hardly.

vōcālis, -e, speaking, tuneful.

voco (1), call, name, summon, invite.

volātus, -ūs, *m.*, flight.

volito (1), fly.

volo (1), fly.

volo, velle, volui, be willing, wish.

volucris, -is, *f.,* bird.
voluntas, -tātis, *f.,* will, goodwill.
volvo, -ere, -vi, volūtum (3), roll *(transitive).*
vorāgo, -inis, *f.,* depth, abyss.
vorax, -ācis, greedy, voracious.
vōs, *pl. of* **tu.**
vōtum, -i, *n.,* vow, prayer, hope, wish, desire.
voveo, -ēre, vōvi, vōtum (2), vow.
vox, vōcis, *f.,* voice.
vulgus, -i, *n.,* crowd, common people.
vulnero (1), wound.
vulnificus, -a, -um, wounding, wound-dealing.
vulnus, -eris, *n.,* wound.
vultus, ·ūs, *m.,* face, countenance, look.